The Dallas Symphony Cookbook

The Dallas Symphony Cookbook

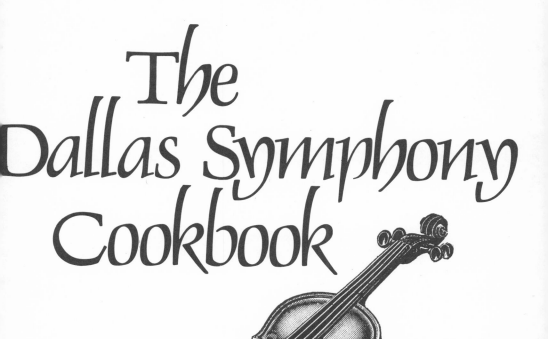

 Junior Group,
Dallas Symphony Orchestra League

Dallas, Texas

Additional copies may be ordered for $12.95 per book plus $2.00 postage and handling. Texas residents add $.65 sales tax. Send check to the following address:

Junior Group Publications
P.O. Box 8472
Dallas, Texas 75205

Library of Congress Catalogue Card #83-080933
ISBN 0-9611216-0-2
First Printing   October 1983   10,000

Printed in U.S.A. by
Hart Graphics, Inc.
8000 Shoal Creek Blvd.
Austin, Texas 78758

FOREWORD

Our greatest gifts to others and to ourselves are those that express and reveal our creativity - that most personal component through which our inner selves are exposed. Composers past and present sought to envelop us in the full gamut of musical expression. Today's creative cook, with a fraction of the talent and time, can orchestrate a stunning performance.

Noted Cookery, first published in 1969 and currently in its sixth printing, set a standard for excellence that we have fully endeavored to meet. It is our hope that *The Dallas Symphony Cookbook* will become a treasured cookbook for special entertaining. We have evaluated and tested over 1,000 recipes and have carefully selected those which elevate the ordinary to the special, and the special to the sublime.

Modern culinary emphasis is toward a light, fresh approach to food and away from heavy sauces and calorie-laden menus. The herb recipes in the book are our tribute to this forward-thinking cuisine. Each herb recipe is designated by the rosemary sprig for easy recognition. We hope you will experiment with and savor the many fine fresh herbs available today.

The Dallas Symphony Cookbook is a culmination of several years' work. Our committee has acquired many cherished friendships, not a few unwanted pounds, and a wealth of different and delicious recipes. Now we are delighted to share our bounty with you.

 This symbol denotes the herb, rosemary, which is used with all recipes using fresh herbs in this cookbook.

COVER PHOTOGRAPH

The photograph which appears on the cover is a visual representation of one evening of special entertaining. Recipes for these dishes may be found in this cookbook on the pages listed below.

Recipes from right to left:

The fresh arrangement of culinary herbs was custom designed by Suzanne's Flowers, Inc. Sentiments expressed by the fresh herbs selected include the following.

Activity - Thyme
Comfort - Comfrey
Cheerfulness - Mint
Constancy - Box
Courage - Borage
Enchantment - Lemon Verbena
Esteem - Sage
Festivity - Parsley
Glory - Bay Laurel
Good Wishes - Basil
Immortality - Tansy
Love - Rose
Loyalty - Rosemary
Luck - Lavendar
Merry Heart - Salad Burnet
Purity - Lilly
Youthfulness - Chives

COOKBOOK COMMITTEE

Mrs. Joe M. Dealey, Jr. (Pam), *Chairman*

Mrs. Kenneth Bardin, Jr. (Melinda)
Mrs. W. Bennett Cullum (Betsy)
Mrs. Richard L. Collier (Leslie)
Ms. Sheryn R. Jones
Mrs. Tim Kirk (Jeannie)
Mrs. John F. Lehman, Jr. (Linda)
Mrs. Michael L. McCullough (JoAnne)
Mrs. James B. Scott (Janet)

Special thanks to our herb consultant
Mrs. William L. Furneaux (Lane)

The Cookbook Committee wishes to thank the members of the Junior Group for submitting and testing more than 1000 wonderful recipes for this cookbook. We regret that all recipes could not be included.

Our sincere thanks to those who contributed
their time and talents.

Art Director — Bob Haydon
Photographer — Doug Tomlinson
Food Stylist — Marilyn Wyrick Ingram

Special Thanks
Jean LaFont
Executive Chef, Vaccaro Restaurants of Dallas

Contents

Appetizers and Beverages

CAMEMBERT EN CROÛTE   Serves 6

½ cup flour, sifted
⅛ teaspoon salt
2 ounces cream cheese
4 tablespoons butter
1 (7-8 oz.) round
  Camembert cheese
1 egg yolk
2 teaspoons water

Make pastry day before. Sift flour with salt. Cut in cream cheese and butter until mixture resembles coarse crumbs. Shape into ball; flatten slightly. Wrap in plastic, refrigerate overnight. Three hours before serving, roll out dough to ⅛-inch thickness. Cut out 7-inch circle. Place on baking sheet. Set Camembert in center of circle. Bring pastry up around side and ½-inch over top of cheese. Press smooth. From dough trimmings, cut circle to fit top of cheese. Beat egg yolk and water. Brush on pastry rim around top edge of cheese. Place pastry circle on top. Cut two strips 5-inches long and ½-inch wide and 3 "leaves" from remaining pastry. Roll each strip to resemble a rosebud. Place with leaves in center of pastry. Brush with egg mixture. Refrigerate at least 1 hour before baking. Bake at 425⁰ for 20 minutes or until brown. Cool at room temperature 30 minutes. Cut into wedges.
  Mrs. Joseph F. McKinney (Clare)

CRUSTLESS QUICHE SQUARES   Yields 4 dozen

½ cup flour
1 teaspoon baking
  powder
¼ teaspoon salt
8 eggs, well beaten
3 cups grated Monterey
  Jack cheese
1½ cups cottage cheese
2 (4 oz.) cans chopped
  green chilies, drained

Preheat oven to 350⁰. Combine flour, baking powder, and salt. Add eggs and mix well. Fold in cheeses and chilies. Turn into a greased 9 x 13-inch ovenproof dish. Bake 40 minutes. Remove from oven; let stand 10 minutes. Cut in small squares. Serve hot.
  Mrs. Paul A. Lantrip (Mae)

BUTTERNUT BRIE   Serves 12

¾ cup butter, softened
⅔ cup chopped pecans
5-6 tablespoons cognac
½ teaspoon lemon juice
⅛ teaspoon salt
¼ teaspoon red pepper
2 (4-inch) wedges Brie

Mix butter, pecans, cognac, lemon juice, salt, and red pepper together. Remove crust from cheese wedge, covering with butternut mixture. Chill 5 minutes. Remove crust from remaining wedge; place on top of first wedge. Coat top and sides with butternut mixture. Refrigerate; let stand at room temperature 1 hour before serving with crisp crackers or French bread.

Mrs. Charles R. Gibbs (Harriett)

VEGETABLE CHEESE CAKE   Serves 10-12

6 ounces cheese crackers, crushed
2 tablespoons butter, melted
1 Bell pepper (green), minced
1 rib celery, chopped
1 small onion, minced
½ cup chopped green olives
2 (8 oz.) packages cream cheese, softened
2 tablespoons lemon juice
¼ teaspoon paprika
½ teaspoon salt
1 teaspoon hot pepper sauce
Pimiento
Ripe olives
Fresh parsley

Combine crackers and butter; spread in bottom of springform pan. Blend bell pepper, celery, onion, and olives; drain thoroughly. Add remaining ingredients and blend until creamy. Pour mixture into pan and refrigerate. Unmold, decorate with pimiento, ripe olives, and fresh parsley. Serve with wheat crackers. Best if made a day ahead.

Mrs. Tim Kirk (Jeannie)

Omit crust and stuff into cherry tomatoes. Garnish with capers.

OLIVE CHEESE TOASTS

Yields 64

2 cups grated Cheddar
cheese
1 cup mayonnaise
1 (6 oz.) can chopped
ripe olives
1½ cups chopped green
onions
1 teaspoon curry powder
½ teaspoon salt
1 teaspoon pepper
8 English muffins

Preheat oven to 375°. Combine all
ingredients mixing well. Spread
generously on English muffins. May be
frozen at this point. Bake until
browned. Cut into fourths.

Mrs. Tony Goolsby (Toppy)

*Warm and toasty; pair with soup on a
chilly day.*

GRUYÈRE ROLL-UPS

Yields 5 dozen

Crêpes:
1 cup biscuit mix
1 egg
1 cup milk
1 tablespoon brandy

Combine all ingredients and beat until
smooth. Spoon 2 tablespoons batter into
hot, lightly greased 6 or 7-inch crêpe
pan. Rotate pan until batter covers
bottom. Bake until bubbles appear.
Gently loosen edge; turn and bake other
side.

Filling:
4 tablespoons butter
4 tablespoons flour
2 cups whipping cream
2 tablespoons dry white
wine
8 ounces Gruyère cheese,
grated
2 tablespoons minced
onion
Nutmeg and Accent to
taste

Cook gently until thick and smooth.
Spread crêpes with filling. Roll and
refrigerate until thoroughly chilled. Cut
each roll into 4 or 5 pieces and then dip
into egg, beaten with a little water. Roll
in finely crushed cracker or breadcrumbs.
Roll-ups may be made in advance and
frozen. Thaw 30 minutes then deep-fry
until brown.

DIVINE CHEESE MOUSSE
Yields 3 cups

1 envelope unflavored
  gelatin
¼ cup cold water
2½ ounces Camembert
  cheese
3¾ ounces Roquefort
  cheese
1 teaspoon worcestershire
  sauce
1 egg, separated
½ cup whipping cream,
  whipped
Crab or shrimp (optional
  garnish)

Soften gelatin in water. Set in hot
water bath and heat until dissolved.
Blend cheeses, worcestershire, and egg
yolk into gelatin. Whip egg white
stiffly and fold into whipped cream;
fold into cheese mixture. Mold in 3-cup
mold or individual ramekins. Chill until
set. Garnish with crab or shrimp, if
desired. Serve with French bread.

HUNGARIAN CHEESE PÂTÉ
Yields 2 cups

1 (8 oz.) package cream
  cheese
½ cup finely chopped
  onion
½-1 clove garlic, finely
  minced
1 teaspoon pepper
1 teaspoon seasoning salt
1 cup farmers cheese or
  cottage cheese, drained
½ cup chopped parsley
Chopped parsley
Cracked pepper

Blend all ingredients except farmers
cheese and parsley until smooth. Add
farmers cheese and parsley; blend briefly
and chill. Shape mixture into ball or
log. Roll pâté in additional parsley or
cracked pepper. Make in advance to
blend flavors.

Mrs. Richard D. Eiseman (Louise)

CHEESE BISCUITS

Yields 3-4 dozen

2 cups grated sharp
  Cheddar cheese
1 cup butter, softened
1 teaspoon worcestershire
  sauce
½ teaspoon salt
1 cup chopped pecans
½ teaspoon red pepper
2¼ cups flour

Preheat oven to 425°. Combine cheese, butter, worcestershire, salt, pecans and red pepper. Cut in flour so that a firm dough forms. Pat dough out to a thickness of ½ inch. Cut dough with a small biscuit cutter or drop by heaping teaspoons onto ungreased baking sheets. Bake 12-15 minutes.

Mrs David H. Dial (Phronsie)

BLEU CRAB FONDUE

Serves 12-15

½ cup dry white wine
1 (8 oz.) package cream
  cheese, cubed
8 ounces crabmeat
1 tablespoon minced
  chives
3 ounces bleu cheese,
  crumbled

Pour wine into 1-quart oven-proof dish. Heat until bubbly; add cream cheese. Cook uncovered 1½-2 minutes or until cheese melts, stirring once. Blend in crabmeat and chives; cook uncovered 30 seconds. Gently toss in bleu cheese and heat 1 minute or until fondue is very hot. Use artichoke hearts, apple slices or raw mushroom slices for dipping.

Mrs. Robert A. Fanning (Carolyn)

CHAFING DISH CRAB

A creamy, crab fondue

20 ounces cream cheese,
  softened
Pepper
3 tablespoons lemon juice
1 teaspoon picante sauce
1 teaspoon worcestershire
  sauce
1 pound lump crabmeat
¾ cup slivered almonds,
  lightly browned in
  butter

Whip cream cheese in double boiler. Add seasonings, mixing well. Stir in crabmeat and almonds. Serve hot in chafing dish with crackers or toast rounds.

Mrs. Charles R. Gibbs (Harriett)

OLIVE RELISH

Yields 1 cup

1 (4 oz.) can chopped
  ripe olives
1 (4 oz.) can chopped
  green chilies
2 tomatoes, seeded and
  chopped
1 bunch green onions,
  chopped
3 cloves garlic, chopped
3 tablespoons olive oil
2 tablespoons red wine
  vinegar
1 teaspoon pepper

Combine all ingredients. Refrigerate overnight. Serve with corn chips. This will keep in refrigerator 2 weeks.

With 1900 as its official year of birth, the Dallas Symphony is one of the six oldest major American Symphony orchestras. The Philadelphia Orchestra was organized the same year, only New York, Boston, Chicago and St. Louis have longer orchestral histories. The Symphony is certainly the oldest of the major cultural institutions in Dallas.

OYSTER LOAF

Serves 12

2 (8 oz.) packages cream
  cheese, softened
½ cup mayonnaise
2 teaspoons hot pepper
  sauce
1 tablespoon
  worcestershire sauce
Milk
2 (3¾ oz.) cans smoked
  oysters, drained
Chopped parsley
Pumpernickel bread

Combine cheese, mayonnaise, hot pepper sauce, worcestershire, and enough milk to make pliable but not too soft. Add oysters; shape and refrigerate. Best if prepared several days in advance. Before serving, cover with parsley. Serve with pumpernickel bread cut into fourths.

SALAMI CORNUCOPIAS

(Italian parsley, onion or garlic chives, dill weed, sage)

**12 large slices salami*,
    halved**
**11 ounces cream cheese,
    softened**
**2 tablespoons chopped
    fresh Italian parsley**
**2 tablespoons chopped
    fresh onion or garlic
    chives**
**2 tablespoons chopped
    fresh dill weed**
**⅛ teaspoon chopped,
    tender, fresh sage leaves**
¼ teaspoon salt
½ teaspoon lemon juice
2 dashes hot pepper sauce
**2 dashes worcestershire
    sauce**

Twist each half circle of salami around finger to form tiny cones; press edges firmly to seal. Combine cream cheese, herbs, and seasonings with wooden spoon and put in pastry bag with fluted tip. Fill salami cones and refrigerate at least 1 hour before serving.

Mrs. B. A. Lamun (Linda)

*Salami slices should be 4 inches in diameter and about 1/16-inch thick.

Try this filling with celery or raw vegetables.

The Dallas Symphony Orchestra traces its beginnings to May 12, 1900, when a 40-member ensemble of the Dallas Symphony Club presented a concert at Turner Hall, at the site of the present Masonic Temple. The conductor, Hans Kreissig, was also the piano soloist. Only five members of the group were professional musicians.

ROSEMARY WALNUTS

(Rosemary)

**1 tablespoon butter,
    melted**
**1 teaspoon crushed fresh
    rosemary**
½ teaspoon salt
¼ teaspoon paprika
1 cup walnuts

Preheat oven to 350°. Mix all ingredients together; spread on baking sheet. Bake 10 minutes. Do not let burn. Serve hot.

Adrienne Lind

PICADO

5 avocados, peeled and
chopped
Juice of 2½ lemons
5 zucchini, peeled and
chopped
2 cups sour cream
1 red onion, finely
chopped
Garlic salt
Pepper

Toss avocados with lemon juice. Mix
remaining ingredients, then add
avocados. Refrigerate several hours or
overnight to blend flavors. Serve cold or
warm with tortilla chips.

Mrs. William Cravens (Janis)

THISTLE DIP   Yields 2 cups

1 (14½ oz.) can artichoke
hearts, drained and
chopped
7 slices bacon, cooked
and crumbled
2 tablespoons chopped
chives
1½ cups mayonnaise

Mix all ingredients and serve cold with
tostada chips or potato chips.

Mrs. James B. Scott (Janet)

SOY GINGER DIP   Yields 2 cups

½ cup finely chopped
green onion
⅓ cup finely chopped
parsley
2 (8 oz.) cans water
chestnuts, drained and
coarsely chopped
2 cups mayonnaise
2 cups sour cream
1 (5 oz.) jar crystallized
ginger, finely chopped
2 tablespoons soy sauce

Mix all ingredients together. Prepare a
day ahead and chill. Serve with wheat
crackers.

Mrs. James B. Montgomery (Nancy)

REMOULADE DIP

Yields 1½ cups

4 tablespoons oil
1 teaspoon salt
½ teaspoon paprika
4 small green onions, minced
2 tablespoons tarragon vinegar
2 tablespoons Creole mustard
4 hearts of celery, finely chopped
⅔ cup mayonnaise
Garlic salt
Pepper

Combine all ingredients, mixing well. Use crab or shrimp for dipping.

Mrs. Lawrence S. Barzune (Dolores)

SPINACH-YOGURT DIP

Yields 4 dozen

⅓ cup chopped onion
2 tablespoons chopped walnuts
2 tablespoons butter, melted
1 (10 oz.) package frozen chopped spinach, thawed and drained well
1 (8 oz.) container plain yogurt
½ teaspoon salt
½ teaspoon nutmeg
⅛ teaspoon pepper
1 clove garlic, minced
¼ teaspoon seasoning salt

Sauté onion and walnuts in butter, 3 minutes, or until onion is tender. Stir in spinach; cook 5 minutes; remove from heat. Combine yogurt and seasonings in bowl. Stir in spinach mixture. Chill covered 1-2 hours, allowing flavors to blend. To serve, spread crackers with spinach-yogurt mixture or serve with thinly sliced zucchini, yellow squash and carrot sticks.

Mrs. Paul A. Lantrip (Mae)

CAPONATINA

Yields 2 quarts

1 large onion, chopped
1 cup chopped celery
½ cup olive oil
2 pounds eggplant, unpeeled, cut into 1-inch cubes
1 (13½ oz.) can tomato paste
1 cup water
1 (16 oz.) jar stuffed green olives, drained
1 (2 oz.) jar unsalted capers, drained
Salt
Pepper
1½-2 tablespoons sugar
¼ cup wine vinegar

Sauté onion and celery in olive oil until almost tender; remove and reserve. In same saucepan, sauté eggplant until lightly brown; remove. Add tomato paste and water to saucepan; cook over medium heat stirring until dissolved. Add olives, capers, eggplant, onion, celery, salt, and pepper. Bring mixture to boil over high heat. Lower heat; simmer 5 minutes. Add sugar and vinegar. Stir and cook 30 seconds. Remove from heat. Serve as an antipasto or with meat or fowl.

Mrs. David W. Gleeson (Sharon)

Caponatina may be packed in sterilized jars and given as Christmas gifts or may be kept covered in refrigerator 4 weeks.

CAVIAR TREATS

Yields 4 dozen

4 dozen tiny new potatoes
Salt
2 cups sour cream
¼ cup chopped chives
1 (8 oz.) jar caviar

Cover new potatoes with water and boil until just tender, not mushy. Drain and cool. Scoop out cavity in each potato leaving enough of pulp for support. Sprinkle with salt. Combine sour cream and chives; fill each cavity ¾ full with mixture. Top with a generous serving of caviar.

Mrs. Richard A. Trimble (Patricia)

Potato shells may be fried and stuffed with potato pulp-cream cheese mixture before topping with caviar.

MUSHROOM PÂTÉ
(Thyme)

½ pound mushrooms, chopped
1 teaspoon chopped fresh thyme
1-2 tablespoons butter
Salt
Pepper
Butter

Sauté slowly mushrooms and thyme in butter. Lift mushrooms from pan with slotted spoon and mince finely. Boil liquid in pan and reduce to 1-2 tablespoons. Stir in mushrooms, salt, and pepper; pack into dish for serving. When mushrooms are cold, melt butter and pour over mushrooms covering completely. When set, cover and refrigerate.

Mrs. Elizabeth Peplow

Mrs. Peplow recently participated in the planning and planting of a herb garden at Westminster Abbey on the site believed to have been the original infirmary garden.

OPAL BASIL
MARINATED MUSHROOMS   Yields 2 (½ cup) servings
(Basil, garlic)

½ pound fresh mushrooms, sliced
⅔ cup salad oil
⅓ cup Opal Basil Vinegar (or red wine vinegar mixed with 1 tablespoon fresh chopped basil or 1 teaspoon dried basil)
1 teaspoon salt
1 teaspoon sugar
½ teaspoon pepper
1 clove garlic, crushed

Place mushrooms in a bowl. Combine remaining ingredients in a jar and shake vigorously. Cover the mushrooms with the dressing; marinate overnight in refrigerator. Use as is or in a tossed green salad.

Mrs. James M. Plumlee (Mary)

Note: This is like a basic oil and vinegar dressing. Keeps indefinitely in the refrigerator. Bleu cheese may be added for a variation. This recipe is a good marinade for all vegetables.

23

MUSHROOM ALMOND PÂTÉ — Yields 2½-3 cups

1 bunch green onions,
  chopped
1 small clove garlic,
  chopped
½ pound mushrooms,
  coarsely chopped
½ teaspoon salt
½ teaspoon tarragon
⅛ teaspoon nutmeg
⅛ teaspoon white pepper
4 tablespoons butter
6 ounces sliced almonds,
  toasted and coarsely
  chopped
¼ cup white wine
2 tablespoons whipping
  cream
½ cup almonds

Combine onion, garlic, mushrooms, salt, tarragon, nutmeg, and pepper. Sauté mixture in butter until most of liquid has evaporated. Reserve 2 tablespoons of coarsely chopped almonds. Pulverize remaining almonds until they reach paste consistency. Add mushroom mixture, wine, and cream. Blend until smooth. Add reserved 2 tablespoons of almonds. Transfer to dish; cover; and chill. Mound pâté on serving plate. Garnish with almonds and serve with sliced French bread.

ROQUEFORT ASPARAGUS WRAPS — Yields 90

8 ounces bleu cheese or
  Roquefort cheese
1 (8 oz.) package cream
  cheese, softened
1 tablespoon mayonnaise
1 egg, beaten
30 slices sandwich bread,
  crust removed
30 asparagus spears,
  cooked
Grated Parmesan cheese
½ cup butter, melted
Paprika

Preheat oven to 350°. Combine bleu cheese, cream cheese, mayonnaise, and egg; blend until smooth. Roll bread out. Spread each slice with cheese mixture. Top each with 1 asparagus stalk; cut to fit bread if necessary. Sprinkle with Parmesan cheese; roll and dip in melted butter dusting with paprika. May be frozen at this point. Cut each roll into 3 pieces. Bake 15 minutes or until brown.
Mrs. Kevin A. Scott (Alice)

TANGY ARTICHOKE HEARTS
Serves 4

1 (3 oz.) package cream
cheese, softened
1 cup bleu cheese
dressing
¼ cup vermouth
1 teaspoon lemon juice
1 (14½ oz.) can
artichoke hearts, rinsed
and drained
2 tablespoons Parmesan
cheese

Preheat oven to 350⁰. Combine cream
cheese, bleu cheese dressing, vermouth,
and lemon juice. Add artichoke hearts
to mixture. Fill ramekins ¾ full.
Sprinkle tops with Parmesan cheese.
Place ramekins on baking sheet and
bake 35-40 minutes. Cool slightly.

CHICKEN LIVER PÂTÉ
WITH CURRANTS
Yields 3 cups

1 pound chicken livers
Salt
Peppercorns
1 stalk celery, chopped
2-3 sprigs parsley
½ teaspoon red pepper
1 cup butter
1 small onion, chopped
2 teaspoons dry mustard
½ teaspoon ground
cloves
1 clove garlic
2 tablespoons brandy
½ teaspoon nutmeg
¾ cup currants

Simmer livers 10-14 minutes in water
(to cover), which has been seasoned
with salt, peppercorns, celery, and
parsley. Drain; purée livers with red
pepper, butter, onion, mustard, cloves,
garlic, brandy, and nutmeg. After
ingredients are well blended, fold in
currants. Chill in 3-cup mold.

Ms. Barbara Brown

CALIFORNIA CAVIAR SOUFFLÉ   Serves 2

4 tablespoons butter,
  melted
2 tablespoons flour
½ teaspoon salt
⅛ teaspoon red pepper
1 cup hot milk
1 cup grated Monterey
  Jack cheese
4 eggs, separated
4 ounces black or red
  caviar

Preheat oven to 325⁰. Combine butter, flour, salt, and red pepper; cook gently over moderate heat 2 minutes. Add milk; stir until smooth. Add cheese; cook until blended. Beat egg yolks; blend into sauce. Beat egg whites until stiff; fold into sauce. Butter a 2-quart soufflé dish; pour in half of mixture. Put half of caviar in center. Fold remaining caviar into remaining soufflé mixture; pour into dish. Bake 30 minutes. Serve immediately.

GREEN CHILI
SAUSAGE PINWHEELS   Yields 30 rolls

½ cup butter, melted
4½ cups biscuit baking
  mix
1 cup milk
1 pound regular pork
  sausage
1 pound hot pork sausage
5 (4 oz.) cans chopped
  green chilies

Preheat oven to 400⁰. Cut butter into biscuit mix; add milk and stir. Refrigerate 30 minutes. Combine sausages and green chilies; let stand at room temperature. Divide dough in half. Roll out each piece into large rectangle ¼-inch thick. Spread half of sausage mixture over each piece of dough; roll in jellyroll style. Wrap in plastic wrap and freeze 1 hour. Remove from freezer and slice ¼-inch thick. Freeze until ready to use. Place frozen slices on baking sheet and bake 20 minutes.

Mrs. Barton Darrow (Ann)

EGG ROLLS
Yields 10-12

Egg Roll Skins:
¾ cup flour
1 tablespoon cornstarch
1 teaspoon salt
2 eggs, beaten
1½ cup water
⅛ teaspoon sugar
¼ cup oil

Sift flour, cornstarch, and salt into bowl. Add eggs to 1½ cups water; add sugar. Slowly add egg mixture to flour, beating constantly, until batter is smooth. In a 6-inch crêpe pan place 1 teaspoon oil to each egg roll. Pour 3 tablespoons batter into hot skillet, tipping skillet to spread batter over bottom. Fry over medium heat until batter shrinks from sides of skillet. Turn skins and fry 1 minute. Remove and cool.

Egg Roll Filling:
½ cup finely chopped celery
¾ cup shredded cabbage
½ cup water
3 tablespoons oil
¾ cup shrimp, cooked, peeled, and cleaned
¾ cup pork, cooked
4 green onions, finely chopped
¾ cup finely chopped water chestnuts, drained
1 clove garlic, minced
¼ cup soy sauce

Boil celery and cabbage in water until tender; drain. Heat oil in saucepan; add shrimp and pork. Fry 3 minutes, stirring constantly. Add remaining ingredients and fry 5 minutes, stirring constantly.

Cooking Egg Rolls:
4 tablespoons flour
Water
1 recipe egg roll filling
Egg roll skins
½ cup oil

Combine flour and enough water to make thick paste. Place 2-3 tablespoons filling in center of egg roll skin. Fold the two sides together and seal with paste. Fold up each end and seal. Fry in hot oil until golden brown.

Ham, beef, veal, or chicken may be used instead of pork.

27

ORIENTAL PORK NIBBLES   Serves 30

2½ pounds ground pork
  loin
1 (8 oz.) package water
  chestnuts, drained and
  finely chopped
2 cloves garlic, finely
  chopped
10 green onions, finely
  chopped
½ teaspoon salt
Pepper
1 teaspoon sugar
1 tablespoon cornstarch
2 eggs, lightly beaten
Oil

In large bowl, blend all ingredients together until barely mixed. Form into 90-100 walnut-sized balls. Heat oil in deep fryer to 370°. Fry balls until browned. Remove and drain. Serve hot with Sauce Oriental.

Sauce:
2 cups chicken broth
½ cup soy sauce
1½ tablespoons
  cornstarch
2 tablespoons water

In small saucepan, bring broth and soy sauce to a boil; cover. Reduce heat and simmer 20 minutes. Dissolve cornstarch in water; add to mixture. Stir and cook to thicken sauce. Place some of pork balls in chafing dish; pour sauce over and keep warm.

Mrs. Oscar W. Ponder (Evelyn)

TOASTED TORTILLA CHIPS
(Oregano and parlsey)

¼ cup mayonnaise
3 tablespoons chopped
  fresh oregano
3 tablespoons chopped
  fresh parsley
⅛ teaspoon red pepper
½ teaspoon salt
10 flour tortillas

Preheat oven to 300°. Combine mayonnaise, oregano, parsley, red pepper and salt. Spread over tortillas, stack, and cut into 6 wedges. Separate and spread individually on baking sheet; bake 10 minutes or until lightly browned.

Mrs. Pat N. Reagan

OYSTERS ROCKEFELLER
Yields 24

⅔ cup butter
1 (10 oz.) package frozen spinach, cooked and drained
¼ cup finely minced onion
3 tablespoons cooked and finely minced lettuce
¼ cup finely minced celery
½ teaspoon tarragon
½ teaspoon chervil
½ teaspoon anchovy paste
½ teaspoon salt
½ teaspoon white pepper
24 oysters in shells
2 tablespoons Anisette
2 tablespoons cooked and minced bacon
3 tablespoons breadcrumbs
Lemon wedges

Combine butter, spinach, onion, lettuce, celery, tarragon, chervil, anchovy paste, salt, and pepper in saucepan. Cook over low heat 2-3 minutes. Place oysters under broiler approximately 5 minutes; remove and top each oyster with 1 tablespoon sauce, a drizzle of Anisette, bacon, and breadcrumbs. Broil 3-5 minutes until sauce is hot and breadcrumbs are browned. Serve with lemon wedges.

Jane Gentry

SPICY MANGO CHUTNEY
Yields 6 pints

4 pounds ripe mangoes, peeled, seeded, and chopped
2 large onions, chopped
8 ounces fresh gingerroot, peeled and chopped
2 cloves garlic, chopped
3 pounds brown sugar
1 teaspoon red pepper
1 tablespoon salt
4 cups vinegar
2 pounds raisins

Combine all ingredients and refrigerate overnight. In saucepan boil until thick. Pour into hot, sterile jars and seal or pour into clean, non-sterile jars and refrigerate.

Serve over cream cheese.

SALMON MOUSSE WITH VERMOUTH DRESSING

Serves 12

1 (16 oz.) can salmon, drained with liquid reserved for sauce
1 teaspoon salt
¼ teaspoon pepper
⅛ teaspoon nutmeg
⅛ teaspoon red pepper
2 egg whites
2 cups whipping cream
Black caviar or sliced black olives (optional garnish)
Smoked salmon or tiny boiled shrimp (optional garnish)

Preheat oven to 350°. Purée salmon with salt, pepper, nutmeg and red pepper until smooth; beat in egg whites one at a time. Whipping steadily, add cream slowly. Bake in a well-greased loaf pan, covered with buttered wax paper for 30 minutes or until firm. Serve at room temperature or cold with Vermouth Dressing; garnish with caviar and smoked salmon slices formed into rosettes.

Vermouth Dressing:
1 (8 oz.) package cream cheese
1 tablespoon mayonnaise
2 tablespoons reserved salmon liquid
2 tablespoons vermouth
Pepper

Blend until smooth; serve cold.
Mrs. Stephen Sadacca (Sharron)

Hans Kreissig, founder and first conductor of the Dallas Symphony Orchestra, directed the orchestra for five seasons. Pianist, teacher, and conductor, Kreissig was a pioneer in the musical life of Dallas. Born in Breslau, Germany, Kreissig came to New York in 1880, where he became musical director for the Grau light opera company. On tour with the company in 1888, Kreissig visited Dallas, and when the tour company dissolved in Little Rock, Arkansas, Kreissig returned to Dallas. He married a Dallas beauty, and went on to organize the Dallas Symphony Club, which performed its first concert on May 12, 1900.

ALMOND TEA
Serves 8-10

Easy to do for a meeting

3 tea bags
10 tablespoons lemon
   juice
1 tablespoon vanilla
   extract
1 tablespoon almond
   extract
2 cups boiling water
1 cup sugar
4 cups water

Steep tea bags, lemon juice, and extracts in boiling water. Boil sugar in water 5 minutes; combine all ingredients. Serve hot or cold.

AMARETTO EGGNOG
Serves 20

6 egg yolks
½ cup sugar
4 cups milk
¾ cup Amaretto
1 cup whipping cream
2 teaspoons vanilla
   extract (optional)
6 egg whites
1 cup whipping cream

Combine egg yolks, sugar, and milk in saucepan. Beat until smooth; stir in Amaretto. Cook and stir over low heat until mixture thickens and coats spoon. Refrigerate until serving time. Add whipping cream and vanilla. Whip egg whites with whipping cream; gently fold together yolk mixture and egg white mixture in serving bowl.

Mrs. Jack Urish (Dee)

CITRUS SLUSH
Serves 8

1 (6 oz.) can frozen
   lemonade
1 (6 oz.) can frozen
   limeade
1 (6 oz.) can frozen
   orange juice
6 ounces pineapple-
   grapefruit juice
6 ounces vodka (optional)

Combine all ingredients in blender. Fill blender with ice; process until slushy. Serve immediately.

Mrs. John F. Lehman, Jr. (Linda)

BANANA PUNCH   Serves 50

4 cups sugar
6 cups water
1 (12 oz.) can frozen
  orange juice
1 (46 oz.) can pineapple
  juice
3 tablespoons lemon juice
5 ripe bananas
3 (32 oz.) bottles
  gingerale

Combine sugar and water in saucepan; cook over medium heat 3-5 minutes. Stir in juices; freeze in shallow pan. At serving time mash bananas and combine with juice mixture in a punch powl; add gingerale.

Miss Carla Coldwell

CHRISTMAS BUTTERED RUM   Yields 2 pints drink

1 cup butter
½ cup packed brown
  sugar
½ cup powdered sugar,
  sifted
1 tablespoon nutmeg
1 tablespoon cinnamon
1 pint vanilla ice cream,
  softened
Rum
Boiling water

Cream butter, brown sugar, powdered sugar, nutmeg, and cinnamon. Blend in ice cream and freeze. To serve, spoon 4 tablespoons of ice cream mixture into mug. Add 3 tablespoons of rum and ¼ cup boiling water. Stir well.

Mrs. Weldon Maxey (Lana)

COFFEE CREAM PUNCH   Serves 25
Rich and wonderful

1 gallon strong coffee
1½ cups sugar
1 quart whipping cream,
  whipped
2 teaspoons vanilla
  extract
1 gallon vanilla ice cream
Shaved or grated
  chocolate (optional)

Combine coffee and sugar; chill. When ready to serve pour coffee into punch bowl. Add whipped cream flavored with vanilla and add ice cream. May be made in advance and stored in refrigerator.

Mrs. William Cravens (Janis)

Top each cup with a bit of chocolate shavings.

ITALIAN WINE PITCHER

Serves 6-8

Tart and refreshing

3½ cups dry white wine
½ cup cognac or brandy
¼ cup sugar
3 unpeeled lemons, sliced
1 unpeeled orange, sliced
1 green apple, cut into
  wedges
1 (10 oz.) bottle club
  soda, chilled
Ice cubes
Fresh mint (optional)

Combine wine, cognac or brandy, and sugar in pitcher; mix well. Add fruit and chill overnight. Before serving, add club soda; place ice cubes in each wine glass; pour in punch and top with slices of fruit. Add sprigs of fresh mint to each glass.

Mrs. D. Michael Highbaugh (Pat)

MINT PUNCH

Serves 18

Clean, sparkling flavor

2½ cups water
2 cups sugar
10 sprigs fresh mint
Juice of 6 lemons
Juice of 2 oranges

Combine water and sugar in saucepan; boil until slightly thickened. Add mint; cover and steep 20 minutes; strain. Add juices. To serve dilute 1 part mixture with 2 parts water.

Mrs. Bill L. Nelson (Nancy)

Variations: Use undiluted punch to season tea or mix with bourbon or ginger ale.

HOLIDAY PUNCH

Serves 40-50

4 (10 oz.) packages
  frozen strawberries,
  thawed, do not drain
1 cup sugar
4 (25.4 oz.) bottles pink
  sparkling catawba
  grape juice
4 (6 oz.) cans lemonade
  concentrate, thawed
2 (32 oz.) bottles club
  soda

Mix strawberries, sugar, and 1 bottle catawba juice. Let stand 1 hour. Do not strain. Add lemonade concentrate; stir in remaining catawba juice and club soda. Serve in a punch bowl with ice.

Mrs. Oscar W. Ponder (Evelyn)

HERBLOODY MERRIE   Serves 1

(Sweet basil, oregano, garlic, salad burnet)

¾ teaspoon minced fresh
   sweet basil leaves
¼ teaspoon minced fresh
   oregano
½ clove garlic, crushed
¾ cup tomato juice
3 tablespoons Vodka
½ teaspoon
   worcestershire sauce
2 teaspoons lemon juice
Salt
Pepper
1 leaf salad burnet
Basil stalk

Mix all ingredients, except salad burnet, and pour into an 8-ounce glass filled with ice. Float salad burnet leaf and use flower-tipped basil stalk as stirrer.

Mrs. William C. Holton (Betty)

To make a stirrer out of a basil stalk, select a stalk that is long and strong enough, preferably flower-tipped, and harden in water before using.

HILLTOP'S HERBAL WINE PUNCH   Yield 20 cups

(Rose geraniums, lemon verbena, rosemary, borage flowers)

3 cups unsweetened
   pineapple juice
½ cup sugar
2 tablespoons lemon peel
2 teaspoons cassia buds or
   1 (3-inch) cinnamon
   stick
1 teaspoon whole cloves
1 cup rose geranium
   leaves
1 cup fresh lemon
   verbena
Handful of rosemary
   (optional)
4 cups rosé wine
6 cups ginger ale, chilled
2 cups strawberries, sliced
   or blended with wine

Place pineapple juice, sugar, lemon peel, spices, and geranium leaves in saucepan. Stirring occasionally, bring to a boil for 1 minute; remove from heat. Cool to room temperature and strain. Before serving, pour herbed juice mixture into punch bowl. Add wine, ginger ale, and strawberries; stir well to mix. Carefully place prepared ice ring or ice cubes in punch bowl; garnish with borage or other small flowers or petals and herb leaves.

Madalene Hill and Gwen Barclay
Hilltop Herb Farm,
Cleveland, Texas

34

Soups and Salads

ALMOND BISQUE   Serves 8

½ cup chopped onion
½ cup sliced celery
4 tablespoons butter,
  melted
¾ cup pearl barley,
  rinsed
½ pound mushrooms,
  sliced
9 cups beef bouillon
Salt
Pepper
¼ teaspoon thyme
1 clove garlic, minced
1 bay leaf
½ cup almonds, toasted
  and finely ground
¼ cup dry sherry
1 cup whipping cream
2 tablespoons minced
  parsley

Sauté onion and celery in butter until limp; add barley and sauté 10 minutes until lightly browned. Add mushrooms, bouillon, salt, pepper, thyme, garlic, and bay leaf. Bring to boil; simmer 45-50 minutes, or until barley is tender. Mix in almonds and sherry; simmer 2 minutes. Stir in cream and parsley. Simmer several minutes. Serve hot.

The flavor is round, brown, and creamy.

Try this excellent soup as a formal first course to a meal of veal roast or simply-sauced veal chops, crisp asparagus spears, and Carrot Purée. Serve French Apple Tart for dessert and imagine yourself on vacation in provincial France. Don't forget to dim the lights.

ALMOND CRÈME   Serves 6-8

1 small onion, finely
  chopped
3 tablespoons butter,
  melted
3 tablespoons cornstarch
1 cup chicken broth
½ pound almonds,
  blanched and coarsely
  chopped
5 cups chicken broth
Salt
Pepper
1 cup half and half

Sauté onion in butter. Add cornstarch and 1 cup chicken broth. Stir until smooth. Add almonds and remaining 5 cups chicken broth; heat. Add salt, pepper, and half and half; heat.

Mrs. W. Bennett Cullum (Betsy)

BRIE SOUP
Serves 6

French Onion Soup with a fabulous twist

4 large onions, thinly
  sliced
3 tablespoons butter,
  melted
½ teaspoon salt
4 cups beef broth or
  consommé
⅓ cup dry Madeira
4 ounces Brie cheese

Sauté onions in butter. Add salt and cover tightly. Cook over low heat until tender, approximately 15 minutes; do not brown. Add broth and simmer 20 minutes. Add Madeira. Strain, if desired. Dice cheese in bottom of soup cups and cover with hot soup. Stir and serve.

Miss Helen Corbitt

CHEDDAR CHEESE SOUP
Serves 6

¼ cup finely chopped
  onion
½ cup finely chopped
  Bell pepper (green)
¼ cup finely chopped
  carrot
3 cups chicken broth
2 cups milk
5 tablespoons flour
4 tablespoons butter,
  melted
3 cups grated Cheddar
  cheese
Salt
White pepper
Chopped fresh chives
Croutons
Bacon, cooked and
  crumbled
Parsley

Boil onion, Bell pepper, and carrot in chicken broth until tender. Add milk and set aside. In a large saucepan, add flour to butter and stir until well blended. Add stock mixture and cook until smooth. Add cheese, salt, and white pepper, stirring until cheese is completely melted. Serve hot, garnished with chives, croutons, bacon, or parsley.

Mrs. Maurice Bates (Jean)

CAULIFLOWER SOUP   Serves 6-8

¼ cup chopped onion
4 tablespoons butter, melted
4 tablespoons flour
1 small cauliflower, cooked and puréed
2 cups milk
1 teaspoon salt
1 egg yolk
2 tablespoons grated Cheddar cheese
½ cup cooked and crumbled spicy sausage

Sauté onion in butter until transparent; add flour and stir until mixture thickens. Whisk in cauliflower and milk; heat, but do not boil. Whip in salt, egg yolk, and cheese, stirring until slightly thickened. Top with sausage and serve.

Mrs. Ken Ford (Suz)

The cauliflower fluffs when it is whipped!

CHINESE VEGETABLE SOUP   Serves 6

Rich in flavor — low in calories

6-8 cups chicken broth
3 cups shredded cabbage
½ cup julienned carrots
1 cup thinly sliced onion
1 cup julienned celery
1 large tomato peeled, seeded, and chopped
3 tablespoons oil
1 tablespoon salt
¼ teaspoon pepper
¼ teaspoon monosodium glutamate (optional)
1 teaspoon sesame oil
Hot pepper sauce

Boil chicken broth; add cabbage, carrots, onions, and celery. Reduce heat and simmer 15-20 minutes. Sauté tomato in oil; add to soup with salt, pepper, and monosodium glutamate. Cook 3-4 minutes. Add sesame oil and 2 shakes of hot pepper sauce just before serving.

COLD CARROT SOUP WITH AVOCADO   Serves 6

1 cup chopped onion
4 tablespoons butter, melted
4 cups chopped carrots
3 cups chicken broth
1 cup whipping cream
1 teaspoon salt
1 teaspoon chervil
Hot pepper sauce
White pepper
1 avocado, diced

Sauté onions in butter 1 minute. Add carrots and chicken broth. Cover and simmer 30 minutes. Purée and chill. Add remaining ingredients except avocado. Serve very cold with avocado floating in center.

Miss Helen Corbitt

CREAM OF LETTUCE SOUP   Serves 8
Delicate and classically French

2 (1 lb.) heads of lettuce, cored and coarsley chopped
1 onion, sliced
3 tablespoons butter, melted
Salt
Pepper
⅛ teaspoon sugar
¼ cup flour
4½ cups milk
⅛ teaspoon nutmeg
½ cup whipping cream

Cook lettuce in boiling salted water to cover until tender-crisp. Drain, plunge into cold water to stop cooking. Squeeze out excess water. Sauté onion in butter until soft; do not brown. Add lettuce, salt, pepper, and sugar; cook over medium heat until liquid has evaporated. Add flour, stirring constantly; cook 1-2 minutes until bubbly. Add milk and nutmeg; simmer, stirring occasionally, 20 minutes, until lettuce is tender. Season to taste. Purée, add cream and bring to a boil. Serve with croutons.

Anne Willan

Before adding cream, soup may be refrigerated and stored in a covered container 48 hours before serving. To serve, reheat soup and add cream.

CRAB AND BROCCOLI SOUP

Serves 4-6

½ cup chopped onion
3 tablespoons butter, melted
2 tablespoons flour
2 cups milk
2 cups half and half
2 chicken bouillon cubes
½ teaspoon salt
¼ teaspoon thyme
⅛ teaspoon pepper
⅛ teaspoon red pepper
8 ounces crabmeat
1 pound broccoli, cooked and chopped or 1 (10 oz.) package frozen chopped broccoli, cooked and drained

Sauté onion in butter; blend in flour. Add milk and half and half; heat thoroughly, stirring constantly. Dissolve bouillon cubes in hot soup; add seasonings, crab, and broccoli. Heat gently.

Mrs. William L. Overstreet (Sheryl)

CUBAN BLACK BEAN SOUP

Serves 6

1 pound black beans
2 tablespoons salt
5 cloves garlic, peeled
1½ teaspoons cumin
1½ teaspoons oregano
2 tablespoons vinegar
5 ounces olive oil
½ pound onions, finely chopped
½ pound Bell peppers (green), finely chopped
½ cup cooked white rice
2 tablespoons finely chopped onion
2 tablespoons olive oil
2 teaspoons vinegar

Soak beans in water overnight; drain. Cover beans with water; add salt and cook until soft. Crush together garlic, cumin, oregano, and 2 tablespoons vinegar. Heat oil in saucepan; add onions and peppers and sauté until onions are browned. Add garlic and spice mixture. Drain some water off beans before adding them to saucepan; cook slowly. Marinate rice with onion, oil, and 2 teaspoons vinegar. Add 1 heaping tablespoon of this mixture to each serving of bean soup.

Mrs. Kenneth Bardin, Jr. (Melinda)

CUCUMBER VICHYSSOISE   Serves 4-6

A creamy summer luncheon soup

¼ cup chopped onion or
chopped leek
2 tablespoons butter,
melted
2 cups seeded, diced
cucumbers
1 cup chopped watercress
or chopped Romaine
½ cup peeled, finely
chopped potato
2 cups chicken broth
2 sprigs parsley
½ teaspoon salt
½ teaspoon pepper
1 cup whipping cream
Optional garnish:
Chopped chives
Thinly sliced cucumbers
Thinly sliced radishes

Sauté onion in butter until transparent.
Add cucumbers, watercress or Romaine,
potato, chicken broth, parsley, salt, and
pepper. Bring to a boil; simmer 15
minutes. Purée and season to taste.
Chill. Add cream to chilled mixture
when ready to serve. Garnish with
chives, cucumbers, or radishes.

Mrs. Addison Wilson (Susan)

LENTIL SOUP   Serves 8-10

1 cup diced bacon
1 cup chopped onion
1 potato, peeled and cubed
1 cup sliced carrots
3 cups dried lentils
1 cup cooked ham, diced
1 (16 oz.) can tomato
sauce
1 tablespoon garlic
powder
¾ teaspoon white pepper
¾ teaspoon cumin
2 tablespoons salt
⅛ teaspoon oregano
1¼ gallons chicken broth

Use a large stock pot. Sauté bacon and
onions until tender. Add remaining
vegetables, lentils, ham, tomato sauce,
seasonings, and broth. Heat and simmer
until lentils and vegetables are tender.

GAZPACHO
Serves 4

1 (14½ oz.) can tomatoes
1 onion, chopped
1 cucumber, chopped
1 Bell pepper (green), chopped
2 (6 oz.) cans spicy tomato juice
3 tablespoons red wine vinegar
Salt
Pepper

Purée vegetables and tomato juice. Add vinegar, salt, and pepper. Serve cold.

Mrs. Lawrence S. Barzune (Dolores)

Add tequilla to serve at brunch.

GIN-TOMATO SOUP
Serves 4

9 ripe tomatoes, peeled, seeded, and chopped
½ cup tomato juice
1 clove garlic, minced
⅛ teaspoon thyme
⅛ teaspoon basil
⅛ teaspoon paprika
⅛ teaspoon sugar
1 bay leaf
½ teaspoon salt
¼ teaspoon pepper
½ cup chopped onion
8 medium mushrooms, sliced
2 tablespoons butter, melted
3 slices bacon, cooked and crumbled
6 tablespoons gin
1 cup whipping cream
1 ripe tomato, peeled, seeded, and sliced

Simmer tomatoes, tomato juice, garlic, thyme, basil, paprika, sugar, bay leaf, salt, and pepper until tomatoes are soft; purée. In 2-quart saucepan, sauté onion and mushrooms in butter. Add tomato purée and bacon; boil until reduced to ⅓ of its original volume. Add gin and simmer briefly. Stir in cream and heat, but do not boil. Serve hot, garnished with tomato strips.

Mrs. Richard L. Collier (Leslie)

One (10 oz.) can tomato soup with ½ can water may be substituted for tomatoes. Onions and mushrooms may be sautéed in bacon drippings. There is no need to reduce before adding gin and cream.

Curl up in front of a fire with Gin-Tomato Soup, Herb and Cheese Bread, and creamy Frozen Fruit Salad. Indulge yourself.

MUSHROOM CONSOMMÉ   Serves 6-8

½ pound mushrooms,
  finely chopped
3 tablespoons butter,
  melted
3 cups beef consommé
Juice of 1 lemon
2 tablespoons vermouth
1 tablespoon sherry

Sauté mushrooms in butter. Add consommé, lemon juice, vermouth, and sherry. Serve hot.

Mrs. William H. Clark, III (Kerbey)

For a really special occasion, try it with Beef Madeira, barely steamed broccoli spears tossed with oregano, Carrot Terrine, a Caesar salad, and a smashing dessert like Strawberry Party Vacherin.

MUSHROOM SOUP A L'AMBIANCE   Serves 4
More port sweetens the pot

1 tablespoon finely
  chopped shallots
¼ cup clarified butter
¾ pound fresh
  mushrooms, finely
  chopped
2 tablespoons port wine
2 cups milk
2 cups whipping cream
1 tablespoon butter,
  softened
1 tablespoon flour
Salt
Pepper

Sauté shallots in butter 2 minutes. Add mushrooms and sauté until most of the liquid is gone. Stir in port and cook until well absorbed. Add milk and cream. Bring to a boil and reduce heat to a simmer; cook 10 minutes. Form a beurre manié by kneading together the softened butter and flour into a walnut-sized ball. Season with salt and pepper. Thicken by whisking in small pieces of buerre manié. Serve hot.

L'Ambiance Restaurant

To clarify butter, place in small saucepan and melt over low heat. Spoon off the foamy residue that forms on top and pour clarified butter into a container. Discard residue left in bottom of saucepan.

PEACH SOUP
Serves 8

4 cups peeled and sliced
  peaches
2 cups water
⅓-½ cup sugar
2 cups white wine
1 cinnamon stick
2 tablespoons lemon juice
⅛ teaspoon almond
  extract
Lemon slices

In saucepan combine peaches, water, sugar, wine, and cinnamon. Cover and simmer 30 minutes or until peaches are soft. Discard cinnamon stick. Purée peaches and liquid. Add lemon juice and almond extract. Garnish with lemon slices at serving time. Serve hot or cold.

Mrs. Neal Sklaver (Rebecca)

Drink this in goblets and follow it with Chicken Avocado Salad and sweet muffins. Round out the menu with Boccone Dolce, and send everyone home with the recipes or you'll never be forgiven.

SEVEN BEAN SOUP
Serves 6-8

2 cups mixed dried
  beans, 7 different kinds
2½-3 quarts water
1 pound cubed stew
  meat, browned
2 onions, chopped
1 clove garlic, minced
2 (14½ oz.) cans
  tomatoes
Salt
Pepper
1 teaspoon sweet basil
1 teaspoon oregano
1 cup noodles or barley
Grated Parmesan cheese

Soak beans in water overnight; drain; add water, meat, onions, garlic, tomatoes, salt, and pepper. Simmer 2½ hours. Add basil, oregano, and noodles or barley; simmer 30 minutes. To serve sprinkle with Parmesan cheese.

Mrs. Robert A. Zamorano (Sharon)

Layer the beans in a jar, write out the recipe, and please every family on your Christmas list.

SNAPPER SOUP   Serves 4

½ cup chopped onion
½ cup chopped celery
2 tablespoons butter,
   melted
1 cup chopped Bell
   pepper (green)
4 cups fish stock or clam
   juice
1 teaspoon worcestershire
   sauce
½ cup dry sherry
1 cup skinned, diced,
   raw red snapper
2 cups tomato sauce
4 cups brown sauce,
   homemade or packaged
Salt
Pepper
1 cup dry sherry

Sauté onion, celery, and pepper in butter until soft. Add fish stock, worcestershire, and sherry; simmer 25 minutes. Add snapper and simmer 10 minutes. Add tomato sauce and brown sauce; simmer 5 minutes. Season to taste with salt and pepper. Add ¼ cup sherry to each bowl of soup at serving time. Serve hot.

STRACCIATELLA   Serves 4
Italian egg drop soup

2 eggs, lightly beaten
2 tablespoons grated
   Parmesan cheese
2 teaspoons finely
   chopped parsley
⅛ teaspoon nutmeg
⅛ teaspoon salt
1 quart chicken broth
Salt
Pepper

Combine eggs, cheese, parsley, nutmeg, and salt. In 3-quart saucepan bring chicken broth to a boil. Add egg mixture; simmer 2-3 minutes whisking gently and constantly. The egg mixture will form tiny flakes in stock. Season to taste.

Mrs. K. C. Kinney (Barbara)

CREAMY ZUCCHINI SOUP

Serves 8

1½ pounds zucchini,
    sliced
1 tablespoon salt
1 onion, chopped
2 tablespoons butter
2 cloves garlic, minced
2 tablespoons fresh basil,
    chopped
¾ teaspoon white pepper
2 cups chicken broth
2 cups whipping cream
1 cup sour cream
2 green onions, chopped

In a colander toss zucchini with salt; press down with a plate and allow to drain 1 hour. Rinse and squeeze dry. Sauté onion in butter until translucent; add garlic, basil, and pepper and cook 1 minute. Stir in chicken broth and zucchini; bring to a simmer and cook until the zucchini is very tender, 15 to 20 minutes. Cool and purée with whipping cream and sour cream. Season to taste. Serve cold garnished with chopped green onion.

Mrs. William L. Overstreet (Sheryl)

SYMPHONY HERB SOUP

Serves 4

(Chives, chervil, French tarragon)

2 onions, diced
½ pound leeks, chopped
1 pint chicken broth or 1
    chicken bouillon cube
2 tablespoons butter
1 pound potatoes, peeled
    and diced
2 tablespoons fresh
    chives, blanched and
    chopped
2 tablespoons fresh
    chervil, blanched and
    chopped
2 tablespoons fresh
    French tarragon,
    blanched and chopped
½ cup whipping cream
Salt
Pepper

Sweat onions and leeks in saucepan until soft. Add chicken broth and butter; bring to boil. Add diced potatoes and cook 30 minutes. Sprinkle in chopped and blanched herbs. Blend 30 seconds. Finish with cream; season and serve.

Chef John Hornsby

VERMICELLI AND ONION SOUP
Serves 6

4 onions, chopped
2 tablespoons butter, melted
1 cup broken vermicelli
3 tablespoons tomato paste
6 cups chicken broth
Parmesan cheese, grated

Sauté onions in butter until soft. Stir in vermicelli; cook 2 minutes, stirring as needed. Blend in tomato paste and chicken broth. Simmer 10 minutes. Serve with grated Parmesan cheese.

Mrs. James M. Plumlee (Mary)

CAPERED ASPARAGUS SALAD
Serves 6-8

1 avocado, peeled and thinly sliced lengthwise
1 teaspoon lemon juice
24 stalks fresh asparagus, cooked 3 minutes and chilled
1 head red lettuce or 1 bunch watercress
4 slices bacon, cooked and crumbled
1 tablespoon capers

Sprinkle avocado with lemon juice. Arrange asparagus on lettuce or watercress; cover with avocado, bacon, and capers. Serve with dressing.

Dressing:
2 tablespoons lemon juice
⅓ cup oil
½ teaspoon salt
⅛ teaspoon pepper

Mix lemon juice and oil; add salt and pepper.

Miss Helen Corbitt

For more uniform pieces of bacon, freeze and dice bacon before cooking.

Capered Asparagus Salad, Hearts of Palm Salad, Avocado and Carrot Salad, Romaine, Orange, and Watercress Salad, and Hildegarde's Caesar Salad are recommendations for elegant dinners or as separate courses.

48

HILDEGARDE'S CAESAR SALAD

Serves 4-6

Our legacy from a well-known cooking teacher

2 cloves garlic, crushed and finely chopped
½ cup peanut oil or olive oil or combination
1 cup croutons
1 large head Romaine lettuce
½ cup grated Parmesan cheese
¼ cup crumbled Roquefort cheese
Salt
⅛ teaspoon white pepper
1 egg, beaten
4 teaspoons lemon juice
1 tablespoon worcestershire sauce

Place garlic in oil and let steep at least 1 hour. Strain oil; put ¼ cup oil in a saucepan; heat to lukewarm. Add croutons; toss 1 minute. Turn into serving bowl. Strain remaining oil and reserve. Sprinkle cheeses, salt, pepper, and ¼ cup oil over lettuce. Beat egg, lemon juice, and worcestershire sauce together; pour over lettuce and toss. Before serving, pour the reserved oil, (or add extra oil if needed), over salad. Place a sprinkling of croutons on top of each serving.

Mrs. Lawrence R. Herkimer
(Dorothy)

Walter J. Fried, who was concertmaster with the ensemble that performed under Hans Kreissig, was one of the orchestra's guiding lights during its first quarter century. A gifted violinist, a well-known teacher, and a strong leader and organizer in the development of the symphony orchestra in Dallas, Fried served as the orchestra's conductor from 1905 to 1911. In 1911 he voluntarily stepped down from the symphony podium to persuade the more accomplished Carl Venth to conduct. In 1918, Walter Fried once again took up the task of organizing the musicians, whom he continued to lead until his death.

ROMAINE, ORANGE, AND
WATERCRESS SALAD
Serves 4-6

Extraordinary

1 head Romaine lettuce, broken into bite-sized pieces
3-4 navel oranges, peeled, and seeded
1 bunch watercress
4 scallions, chopped

Place Romaine, oranges, watercress, and scallions in a salad bowl. Pour dressing over and toss.

Mustard Cream Dressing:
¾ teaspoon salt
1½ teaspoons Dijon mustard
1¼ teaspoons sugar
1 tablespoon butter, melted and cooled
1 egg, beaten
⅓ cup whipping cream
2½ tablespoons vinegar
⅛-¼ teaspoon pepper
2 tablespoons orange juice

Combine all ingredients in a double boiler over simmering water. Whisk 5 minutes or until mixture thickens. Cover and chill.

HEARTS OF PALM SALAD
Serves 4

Dressing:
5 tablespoons oil
2 tablespoons red wine vinegar
8-10 green onions, white part only, minced
4 radishes, minced
1 (15 oz.) can hearts of palm, drained
1 head Boston lettuce
¼ cup walnut halves

Combine oil, vinegar, onions, and radishes to make dressing. Serve over hearts of palm and walnuts on Boston lettuce leaves.

Mrs. Jane Gentry

For an elegant presentation, use the pale Boston lettuce nestled in a bed of curly escarole, hearts of palm, walnuts, and even a few halved, red grapes for color with a sprinkling of freshly cut chives as a garnish.

50

GREEK SALAD
Serves 4-6

(Basil, garlic)

1 head red or green leaf
  lettuce
1 bunch watercress
½ - 1 red onion, very
  thinly sliced
1 cup sliced fresh
  mushrooms
½ cup crumbled feta
  cheese
12 - 16 cherry tomatoes

Mix together. Pour dressing over salad.
Toss and serve.

Mrs. Jane Gentry

Dressing:
½ cup olive oil
½ cup lemon juice
3 tablespoons finely chopped fresh
  basil
1 clove garlic, minced
Salt
Pepper
2 drops hot pepper sauce

COBB SALAD
Serves 6-8

1 head Romaine lettuce,
  finely chopped
8 slices bacon, cooked
  and crumbled
4 ounces Roquefort
  cheese, crumbled
3 tomatoes, peeled,
  seeded, and diced
2 avocados, peeled and
  diced
2 eggs, hard-boiled and
  finely chopped
4 pimiento strips

Put Romaine lettuce in a salad bowl.
Arrange bacon, cheese, tomatoes,
avocados, eggs, and pimiento over
lettuce. Refrigerate. Toss with dressing
when ready to serve.

Dressing:
¼ cup pear vinegar
½ cup oil
1 teaspoon lemon juice
1 clove garlic, crushed
½ teaspoon salt
⅛ teaspoon pepper

Combine all ingredients.

Miss Helen Corbitt

*Treat yourself and your friends to a
leisurely lunch of Cobb Salad, Creamy
Zucchini Soup and sliced Cracked
Wheat Carrot Bread.*

SPINACH SALAD

1 pound fresh spinach
Sliced water chestnuts,
  drained
10 fresh mushrooms,
  sliced
1 pound fresh bean
  sprouts
2-3 green onions, sliced
1 egg, hard-boiled and
  chopped
4-6 slices bacon, cooked
  and crumbled

Combine all ingredients. Pour dressing over salad; toss and serve.

Dressing:
⅓ cup ketchup
½ cup sugar
1 cup oil
¼ cup vinegar
⅛ teaspoon hot pepper
  sauce

Blend all ingredients in a bottle; shake vigorously.

Ms. Joyce Ramey

AVOCADO AND CARROT SALAD

2 avocados, peeled and
  finely diced
3 carrots, peeled and
  finely grated
Fresh spinach

Separately toss avocado and carrots each with half of the dressing; chill. At serving time arrange spinach on serving plates, add a ring of carrots, and mound avocado in the center.

Dressing:
1 teaspoon Dijon mustard
1 tablespoon lemon juice
⅛ teaspoon salt
⅛ teaspoon pepper
¼ cup olive oil

Combine mustard, lemon juice, salt, and pepper; add olive oil gradually. Mix until well blended.

Mrs. W. Bennett Cullum (Betsy)

SUMMER SUNSHINE SALAD
Serves 8

A good alternative to cole slaw

1 pound carrots, thinly sliced and steamed tender-crisp
4 small yellow squash, thinly sliced and steamed tender-crisp
1 onion, thinly sliced and steamed tender-crisp
1 Bell pepper (green), thinly sliced and steamed tender-crisp
1 large tomato, diced

Combine all vegetables. Pour dressing over vegetables; chill overnight. Keeps 1 week in refrigerator; improves with age.

Dressing:
¼ cup sugar
5 tablespoons vinegar
¼ cup oil
¼ cup tomato sauce
1 teaspoon worcestershire sauce
1 teaspoon dry mustard
¼ cup whipping cream
⅓ teaspoon salt
¼ teaspoon pepper

Blend all ingredients and bring to a boil; dress vegetables while still hot.
Mrs. Robert J. Bigham, Jr.
(Barbara)

RAW BROCCOLI SALAD
Serves 12

Crudites par excellence

1 bunch broccoli
⅛ teaspoon salt
⅛ teaspoon pepper
⅓ cup oil
2 tablespoons lemon juice
4 tomatoes, peeled and cut into wedges
½ cup mayonnaise or sour cream
1 teaspoon mustard
Lettuce

Chop flowerets of broccoli very finely. Slice stalks into thin strips. Sprinkle broccoli with salt, pepper, and enough oil to moisten lightly; add lemon juice. Mix well and chill 30 minutes or longer. Add tomatoes; blend mayonnaise or sour cream with mustard; add to vegetables. Mix well. Serve on lettuce leaves.
Dr. Francine Daner

CARROT SLAW

Serves 10

More color and a lot more snap

2 pounds cabbage, finely shredded
3 carrots, finely shredded
½ large red onion, finely diced
2 Bell peppers (green), finely chopped

Combine all ingredients; pour dressing over; chill. Toss well before serving.

Dressing:
1 cup mayonnaise
½ cup Dijon mustard
½ cup beer
2 cloves garlic, minced
1 tablespoon celery seed
½ tablespoon pepper

Blend ingredients together.

OLD FASHIONED POTATO SALAD

Serves 8-10

3 tablespoons vinegar
2 tablespoons oil
2 teaspoons salt
½ teaspoon sugar
2 teaspoons mustard
6 potatoes, peeled, cooked, and cubed
1 tablespoon chopped onion
1½ cups sliced carrots, cooked
4 eggs, hard-boiled and sliced
⅓ cup whipping cream
⅔ cup mayonnaise

Combine vinegar, oil, salt, sugar, and mustard. Stir gently into potatoes; marinate several hours or overnight in refrigerator. Add onion, carrots, and eggs to potato mixture. Combine cream and mayonnaise; blend with vegetable mixture. Chill.

Mrs. June Smith

Old Fashioned Potato Salad cries out for summertime picnics, barbeques, pool parties, and the 4th of July.

POTATO SALAD WITH FRESH HERBS   Serves 8
(Onion chives, curly parsley, sage, thyme, oregano, summer savory)

2 pounds potatoes, boiled,
peeled, and cubed
¼ cup dry white wine,
dry vermouth or
bouillon
¼ cup wine vinegar
½ cup olive oil
1 teaspoon dry mustard
1 teaspoon salt
1 teaspoon sugar
Freshly ground pepper
2 tablespoons chopped
fresh onion chives
2 tablespoons chopped
fresh curley parsley
1½ teaspoons chopped
fresh sage
1½ teaspoons chopped
fresh thyme
1½ teaspoons chopped
fresh oregano
1½ teaspoons chopped
fresh summer savory
4 tablespoons chopped
Bell pepper (green)
Cherry tomatoes (optional)

Pour wine, vinegar, oil, mustard, salt, sugar, and pepper over warm potatoes; toss gently. Add herbs and Bell pepper; toss gently. Serve warm or chilled. Herbs should be added just before serving to preserve their color. Garnish with herbs and cherry tomatoes.

Mrs. Chandler Barkelew (Virginia)

RASPBERRY APPLESAUCE SALAD   Serves 4

1 (3 oz.) package
raspberry gelatin
¾ cup boiling water
¾ cup applesauce
2 (10 oz.) packages
frozen red raspberries,
defrosted and drained
(reserve liquid from 1
package)

Dissolve gelatin in boiling water; cool slightly and add applesauce. Blend in the raspberries and the reserved liquid; pour into a mold and refrigerate until set.

Mrs. Allen E. Cullum (Sissy)

RICE SALAD VINAIGRETTE   Serves 10-12

2 cups rice
2 cups chopped
   mushrooms
5 tablespoons butter,
   melted
¾ cup mayonnaise
15 pitted green olives,
   halved
15 pitted black olives,
   halved
4 (4 oz.) jars marinated
   artichoke hearts,
   drained
1 (8 oz.) can green peas,
   drained
1 (4 oz.) can sliced
   pimiento, drained
2 large tomatoes, cubed
1 orange rind, grated
⅛ teaspoon pepper
Romaine lettuce or
   watercress

Cook rice according to directions; chill. Sauté mushrooms in butter until soft. Add mushrooms, mayonnaise, and ½ cup dressing to rice; toss. Cover; refrigerate overnight. Just before serving, add olives, artichoke hearts, peas, pimiento, tomatoes, orange rind, and pepper. Garnish with lettuce or watercress.

Dressing:
2 teaspoons salt
½ teaspoon pepper
1 teaspoon mustard
1 cup olive oil
¼ cup red wine vinegar

Yields 1⅓ cups
Blend salt, pepper, and mustard; mix in several drops of olive oil. Add several drops of vinegar; blending well. Add remaining oil and vinegar. Store in a covered container; refrigerate. Shake well before using.

Mrs. Joe M. Dealey, Jr. (Pam)

Chicken may be added for a luncheon or light dinner.

Vary this hearty favorite by using brown or wild rice.

COLD ZITI SALAD

Serves 20

A hearty, warm-weather standby

4 quarts water
1½ tablespoons salt
2 tablespoons oil
2 pounds Ziti macaroni
¼ cup milk
½ cup sour cream
1½ cups mayonnaise
2 teaspoons beef bouillon
  powder
½ teaspoon salt
Pepper
1 red onion, chopped
2 tomatoes, chopped
6 sweet pickles, chopped
2 small Bell peppers
  (green), seeded and
  cubed
1 large shallot, minced
2 teaspoons wine vinegar
1 tablespoon pickle juice
¼ cup chopped fresh dill

Bring water to a boil. Add salt, oil, and then Ziti. Boil 10 minutes or until tender, stirring occasionally. Drain; rinse in cold water; drain again. In a bowl toss with enough milk to thoroughly moisten. Mix sour cream and mayonnaise with a whisk until creamy; add bouillon powder, salt, and pepper. Pour over Ziti. Reserve 1 tablespoon of each vegetable for garnish. Add remaining vegetables, vinegar, and pickle juice; mix well. Garnish with remaining vegetables. Top with dill.

Mrs. Melvin L. Wellons (Bettye)

AVOCADO ASPARAGUS MOLD

Serves 10

2 cups chicken broth
3 envelopes unflavored
  gelatin
1 tablespoon sugar
3 tablespoons tarragon
  vinegar
¾ cup Bearnaise sauce
1 (8 oz.) container plain
  yogurt
1 (10 oz.) package frozen
  asparagus, cooked and
  puréed
2 avocados, peeled,
  seeded, and puréed

Bring chicken broth to a boil; dissolve in gelatin and sugar; chill until pratically set. Beat together gelatin, Bearnaise, yogurt, asparagus, and avocado. Turn into a greased 6-cup mold and refrigerate until firm. Serve on a bed of lettuce with a garnish of cooked asparagus spears and cherry tomatoes.

CUCUMBER MOUSSE

Serves 6

1 envelope unflavored
  gelatin
¼ cup water
⅓ cup mayonnaise
1 (8 oz.) container plain
  yogurt
1 teaspoon salt
1 teaspoon worcestershire
  sauce
1½ cups pared, seeded,
  and coarsely grated
  cucumber
Salad greens

Sprinkle gelatin over cold water; let stand 5 minutes. Pour mixture into double boiler and stir over hot water until dissolved. Whisk together mayonnaise, yogurt, salt, and worcestershire sauce. Stir in dissolved gelatin; add cucumber. Turn into six ½-cup molds or 1 large mold. Chill. Unmold and garnish with salad greens.

Mrs. Michael L. McCullough
(Jo Anne)

Yogurt lends a delectable nip. Try this at a dinner buffet paired with a hot or cold roast beef. Garnish mousse with cherry tomatoes, marinated green beans, and shiny black olives. Search out cheddar-filled Gourmet Potatoes and cap the evening with something very chocolate, like Black Forest Cake or Frozen Kahlua Cake.

SOUR CREAM TOMATO ASPIC

Serves 10

1¼ cups tomato juice
1 cup water
1 (6 oz.) package lemon
  gelatin
1 cup sour cream
1 cup mayonnaise
3 tablespoons red wine
  garlic vinegar
1 tablespoon horseradish
1 teaspoon onion salt
5 drops hot pepper sauce

Boil tomato juice and water. Add gelatin; stir until dissolved. Cool. Combine remaining ingredients and add to tomato mixture. Blend quickly and pour into a 6-cup mold. Chill.

Make this in a ring mold and fill the center with Raw Broccoli Salad for good color and flavor.

LORENZO SALAD   Serves 8-10

2 envelopes unflavored
  gelatin
½ cup cold water
1 cup boiling water
12 eggs, hard-boiled and
  finely chopped
1 cup mayonnaise
1½ teaspoons salt
½ teaspoon pepper
1 tablespoon lemon juice
2 tablespoons chopped
  Bell pepper (green)
2 tablespoons chopped
  pimiento
Salad oil

Sprinkle gelatin over cold water; let stand 10 minutes. Pour boiling water over gelatin and stir until dissolved. Mix eggs, mayonnaise, salt, pepper, lemon juice, Bell pepper, and pimiento until well blended; add dissolved gelatin. Grease a 6-cup mold; pour in egg mixture. Serve with dressing.

Lorenzo Dressing:
¼ cup vinegar
¾ cup oil
1 teaspoon salt
⅛ teaspoon pepper
⅛ teaspoon hot pepper
  sauce
⅓ cup ketchup
½ cup finely chopped
  parsley
½ teaspoon mustard
2 teaspoons
  worcestershire sauce

Combine all ingredients.

Serve with cold cuts, Raw Broccoli Salad, and Heavenly Bran Muffins.

The third conductor of the Dallas Symphony was Carl Venth. As an orchestral musician, Venth was conducted by both Richard Wagner and Verdi. With his iron-grey hair and his long-tailed coat, Carl Venth was considered the very model of the maestro when he took over the Dallas Symphony in 1911. So great was the improvement in the music-making abilities of the Symphony under Venth that critics flatteringly compared him to a Svengali.

FROZEN FRUIT SALAD   Serves 12
Creamy and delightful

1 (8 oz.) package cream
  cheese
1 cup mayonnaise
¼ cup pineapple juice
¼ cup sugar
1 cup whipping cream,
  whipped
2 (8 oz.) cans pineapple
  chunks, drained
2 (11 oz.) cans mandarin
  oranges, drained
1 cup maraschino
  cherries
1 (16 oz.) can Royal
  Anne cherries, seeded
  and drained
1 cup coarsely chopped
  pecans

Blend cream cheese, mayonnaise, pineapple juice, sugar, and cream. Add remaining ingredients and pour into a ring mold; freeze overnight. Remove 30 minutes before serving.

Mrs. Joe M. Dealey, Jr. (Pam)

FRESH RHUBARB APPLESAUCE   Serves 6

6 Winesap apples
Baking soda
½ cup light corn syrup
4 rhubarb stalks, washed
  and sliced

Wash apples in baking soda water; rinse well, cut into quarters; remove cores. Cook in large saucepan with syrup and sliced rhubarb 1 hour. Cool; push through a sieve.

Mrs. Marjorie B. Waters

Add dash of cinnamon and red food color if desired.

HERB APPLESAUCE
(Sage)

Serves 6

1 pound apples, peeled,
  cored, and sliced
½ cup water
Salt
Pepper
½ teaspoon sugar
2 pieces lemon peel
  without pith
2 tablespoons butter
1 tablespoon chopped
  fresh sage

Boil apples with water, salt, pepper,
sugar, and lemon peel until soft.
Process; then add butter and sage.
Simmer 10 minutes and serve.

Hereford Herbs

CRANBERRY SALAD

Serves 8

2 cups ground
  cranberries
1½ cups sugar
1 cup grapes, seeded and
  chopped
½ cup chopped nuts
1 cup whipping cream,
  whipped

Cover cranberries with sugar and
refrigerate 8-10 hours. Drain; mix with
grapes, nuts, and whipped cream.

Mrs. Wilbur L. Smither (Martha)

MELON MÉLANGE

Serves 6

2 cups water
1 cup sugar
1 teaspoon vanilla extract
⅔ cup Kirsch or orange
  liqueur
3 cups honeydew melon
  balls
1 cup seedless green
  grapes
4 kiwi fruit
Leaf lettuce
Fresh mint (optional)

Bring water, sugar, and vanilla to a
boil; simmer 5 minutes. Cool to room
temperature; add liqueur.

Cover honeydew and grapes with liquid
mixture; refrigerate overnight. At
serving time drain fruits; peel and slice
kiwi fruit into half rounds. Arrange
kiwi in a circle on lettuce leaves; fill
center with melons and grapes. Garnish
with sprigs of fresh mint.

PEARS IN
TARRAGON CREAM DRESSING   Serves 8

Dressing:
1 egg
2 tablespoons sugar
4 tablespoons tarragon
 vinegar

Whisk egg until thick. Gradually beat in sugar and then vinegar. Place in double boiler over boiling water and beat until very thick. Chill until needed.

½ cup whipping cream
Salt
Pepper
4 ripe pears, peeled,
 halved, and cored
¼ cup lemon juice
Leaf lettuce
Paprika

At serving time whip cream and fold into egg mixture; season to taste with salt and pepper. Sprinkle pears on both sides with lemon juice; refrigerate. Arrange lettuce leaves on serving plate; top with pears, rounded side up, and dressing; sprinkle with paprika.

PINEAPPLE GRAPEFRUIT SHELLS   Serves 8
A winter specialty

2 grapefruits, halved
½ envelope unflavored
 gelatin
1 (7 oz.) can crushed
 pineapple, drain and
 reserve liquid
1 (3 oz.) package lemon
 gelatin
Fresh mint

Extract meat from grapefruit halves; reserve. Discard membranes from shells. Mix unflavored gelatin and reserved pineapple juice, dissolving thoroughly. Make lemon gelatin according to directions; add pineapple juice and unflavored gelatin mixture; add pineapple and grapefruit. Fill grapefruit shells. Cut each half into quarters. Garnish with mint.

Mrs. Charles R. Gibbs (Harriett)

CHICKEN AVOCADO SALAD

Serves 6

3 tablespoons lemon juice
2 avocados, peeled and
   diced
 2 cups cubed, cooked
   chicken
1½ cups cooked rice
½ cup chopped celery
2 tablespoons chopped
   onion
6 tablespoons sour cream
6 tablespoons mayonnaise
2 eggs, hard-boiled, 1
   diced and 1 cut in
   rounds
1 teaspoon salt
½ teaspoon pepper
Leaf lettuce or fresh
   spinach
Paprika

Pour lemon juice over avocados. Mix avocados with chicken, rice, celery, onion, sour cream, mayonnaise, diced egg, salt and pepper. Serve on leaf lettuce or spinach; top with egg rounds and sprinkle with paprika.
Mrs. James B. Montgomery (Nancy)

Complement with Romaine, Orange and Watercress Salad, sliced tomatoes, crunchy breadsticks, and Cheesecake with Raspberry Sauce.

CREOLE SHRIMP SALAD

Serves 4

2 pounds shrimp; cooked
   and cleaned
1 cup sliced water
   chestnuts, drained
1 cup mayonnaise
¼ cup minced celery
1¾ teaspoons curry
   powder
2 tablespoons soy sauce
1 tablespoon Creole
   mustard
Lettuce

Combine all ingredients except lettuce. Arrange on lettuce leaves.
Mrs. Charles Rounsaville (Louise)

This spicy salad makes an ideal luncheon choice or first course for a dinner party.

TOMATO AND SHRIMP REMOULADE   Serves 8

1 gallon water
1 (3 oz.) package crab
and shrimp boil
1½ pounds shrimp

Combine water and crab boil; bring to a boil. Add shrimp; cook 1-3 minutes or until shrimp turn opaque and bright pink. Drain and clean. Do not refrigerate.

2 cups large curd cottage
cheese
½ teaspoon salt
1 teaspoon sugar
1½ teaspoons lemon juice
2 teaspoons finely grated
onion
1 clove garlic, minced
½ cup finely chopped
celery
¼ cup finely chopped
parsley
1 teaspoon paprika
¾ teaspoon red pepper
1 teaspoon Dijon mustard
1½ cups mayonnaise
8 tomatoes

Drain cottage cheese in a colander, stirring several times to remove some of the cream. Add remaining ingredients and shrimp; toss lightly. Refrigerate overnight in a covered dish. To serve make 6 slices in tomato ¾ way through. Spread to resemble flower and fill center with shrimp salad.
Mrs. Lloyd A. Lawrence (Judy)

For use as an appetizer chop shrimp before adding to cheese mixture and serve with crackers.

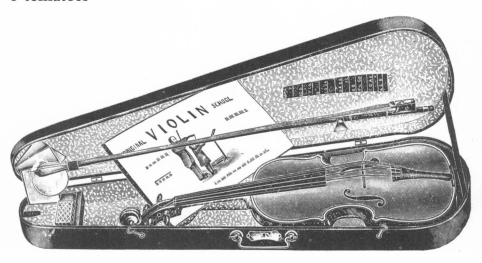

VERMICELLI AND SHRIMP SALAD   Serves 4-6

1 (1 lb.) package
   vermicelli, cooked al
   dente
3 tablespoons lemon juice
3 tablespoons oil
Seasoning salt
1 cup sliced celery
1 Bell pepper (green),
   chopped
1 cup pitted black olives,
   drained
2 pounds shrimp, cooked
   and cleaned
1-1½ cups mayonnaise
Salt
Garlic salt
Pepper
½ teaspoon hot pepper
   sauce

Combine vermicelli, lemon juice, and oil; sprinkle with seasoning salt. Cover and refrigerate 24 hours. Add celery, Bell pepper, black olives, shrimp, mayonnaise, and seasonings; mix well. Serve chilled.

Mrs. Frederick E. Olden (Marti)

Use enough mayonnaise to hold shrimp and vegetables together.

Feature this at a luncheon with Cucumber Vichyssoise, Irish Monkey Bread or Cracked Wheat Carrot loaves.

REFRESHING SALAD DRESSING   Yields 1 cup

¼ cup diced tomato
¼ cup diced cucumber
½ teaspoon minced
   onion
⅛ teaspoon salt
½ cup mayonnaise

Combine all ingredients and chill.

BASIL DRESSING
(Basil, parsley)

2 cloves garlic
1 teaspoon salt
1 red onion, finely
  chopped
½ cup chopped fresh
  basil
¼ cup chopped fresh
  parsley
1 tablespoon lemon juice
⅓ cup olive oil
1 teaspoon pepper

Mash together garlic and salt in mortar with pestal. Combine with remaining ingredients; serve over chilled tomato wedges or slices.

Mrs. Eric H. Dussling

KIRSH FRUIT SALAD DRESSING   Yields 1 cup

2 tablespoons lemon juice
2 tablespoons lime juice
2 tablespoons orange
  juice
⅔ cup sugar
⅓ cup Kirsh

Mix all ingredients together. Pour over any combination of fresh fruit. Marinate 3-4 hours or overnight.

Mrs. Robert T. Gunby, Jr.
(Elizabeth)

CREAMY VINAIGRETTE   Yields 1 cup
Our favorite basic dressing

2 tablespoons minced
  shallots
2 tablespoons Dijon
  mustard
1 tablespoon sour cream
  or créme fraîche
1 tablespoon red wine
  vinegar
⅛ teaspoon salt
Pepper
½ cup oil

Combine shallots, mustard, sour cream, vinegar, salt, and pepper. Add oil slowly while beating constantly until mixture thickens.

DILL SAUCE

Yields 2 cups

(Dill weed, parsley, garlic)

¼ cup chopped fresh dill weed
¼ cup chopped fresh parsley
¼ cup sliced scallions
1 clove garlic, minced
1 cup mayonnaise
2 tablespoons lemon juice
1 tablespoon cognac
½ teaspoon salt
¼ teaspoon pepper
2 tablespoons oil
½ cup sour cream

Blend thoroughly all ingredients, except sour cream, until creamy. Adjust seasonings; add sour cream and mix well. Chill before serving.

Mrs. Lewis L. Shackelford, Jr.

FRANKFURT'S GREEN SAUCE

(Onion chives, parsley, chervil, borage, dill, lemon balm, sorrel)

2 ounces mayonnaise
1 pint sour cream
Juice of 1 lemon
1 hard-boiled egg, chopped
⅛ teaspoon salt
⅛ teaspoon pepper
⅛ teaspoon sugar
1 tablespoon chopped fresh onion chives
1 tablespoon chopped fresh parsley
1 tablespoon chopped fresh chervil
1 tablespoon chopped fresh borage
1 tablespoon chopped fresh dill
1 tablespoon chopped fresh lemon balm
1 tablespoon chopped fresh sorrel

Mix mayonnaise, sour cream, lemon juice, and hard-boiled egg. Add salt, pepper, and stir in herbs; cover and refrigerate.

Mrs. Margit Comploj-Grimmich

Green sauce may be served with hard-boiled eggs, boiled or baked potatoes, beef, or cold asparagus.

CITRUS CREAM DRESSING
Yields 3 cups

1 egg, beaten
¼ cup sugar
1 teaspoon flour
Juice of 1 lemon
Juice of 1 orange
Pineapple juice, enough
  to bring the amount of
  juices to 1 cup
¾ cup whipping cream,
  whipped

In saucepan beat together egg, sugar, and flour. Combine juices, enough to make 1 cup; add to mixture; cook, stirring constantly until thick; chill. Before serving blend equal amounts of whipped cream and dressing base.

Mrs. Frank Deason (Jean)

Dressing base without cream will keep 2 weeks in refrigerator.

This makes a lovely fruit dip especially for bright red strawberries. Just for looks, sprinkle the dressing with julienned orange zest.

FETA DRESSING
Serves 4-6

1 cup mayonnaise
1 clove garlic, minced
4 tablespoons red wine
  vinegar
½ teaspoon oregano
1 tablespoon olive oil
1 cup crumbled feta
  cheese

Combine all ingredients.

Try it in place of a bleu cheese dressing, especially over tomatoes.

FRESH FRUIT-HONEY SALAD DRESSING
Yields 2 cups

½ cup sugar
1 teaspoon dry mustard
1 teaspoon paprika
1 teaspoon celery seed
¼ teaspoon salt
⅓ cup honey
⅓ cup vinegar
1 tablespoon lemon juice
1 teaspoon grated onion
1 cup oil

Mix sugar, mustard, paprika, celery seed, and salt; add honey, vinegar, lemon juice, and onion. Pour oil into mixture very slowly, beating constantly until thick.

Miss Carla Coldwell

HAWAIIAN DRESSING

Yields 2 cups

¼ cup sugar
½ cup honey
½ teaspoon grated onion
3 tablespoons tarragon
  vinegar
1½ tablespoons lemon
  juice
½ cup oil
½ teaspoon dry mustard
½ teaspoon paprika
⅛ teaspoon salt
1 teaspoon poppy seeds
½ teaspoon curry
  powder

Blend all ingredients until smooth.
The Reverend James M. Frensley

Toss with your favorite spinach salad.

GREEN-MINT VINEGAR
(Mint)

1 quart white vinegar
1 cup sugar
2 cups mint leaves
Green food coloring

Bring vinegar and sugar to boil. Mash mint leaves with fork in saucer; put into hot vinegar and simmer 15 minutes. Add green food color sparingly. Strain vinegar and bottle. Use in punch, gelatin or basting leg of lamb.

Barbara Vauderhoff
Jean Givens

HERB VINEGARS

Pack fresh herbs like dill, basil, salad burnet, savory, and tarragon in jar. Pour in white wine vinegar and seal. Leave in a warm place for about 3 weeks; strain into clean bottle. Use in salad dressings, mayonnaise, and vegetables.

Mrs. Lane Furneaux

HERB VINEGAR COMBINATIONS

CARAWAY: Soak 2 tablespoons crushed fresh caraway seed in 1 pint vinegar. Use on slaw.

FOR GREEN SALAD: Cover fresh minced chives, several fresh lovage leaves, savory, and a sprig of marjoram with vinegar.

FOR VEGETABLE SALAD: Combine fresh parsley, fresh oregano, fresh thyme, and a clove of garlic with vinegar.

FOR FRUIT SALAD: Combine mint (anise mint, if available), sweet cecily, angelica, and 1 clove garlic with vinegar. The combination makes a delicious French dressing for fruit salad.

Barbara Vanderhoff
Jean Givens

Hungarian-born Antal Dorati arrived in Dallas in 1945 to revive the Dallas Symphony and make it for the first time a major professional ensemble. In essence, Dorati rebuilt the DSO from the ground up, using only professional musicians, who were paid union scale wages. An intense, demanding conductor, Dorati brought new excitement to the concert hall in Dallas. He also brought some of the world's most accomplished soloists to perform with the DSO—musicians such as Menuhin, Piatigorsky, Heifetz, and Serkin. A mere six weeks after the DSO's first Dorati-led concert, the Symphony was signed for a series of recordings with RCA Victor; amazingly, the DSO's first record, Bartok's Violin Concerto with Yehudi Menuhin as soloist, won the "Grammy" award in 1946. When Dorati left Dallas in 1949 to accept a new post in Minneapolis, he left behind a Symphony that has become an important cultural institution.

Entrées

FETTUCCINE ALLA PESCATORA   Serves 4-6
Pasta with Fresh Clams, Oysters, and Langoustine

1 pound butter
4 cloves garlic, minced
3 shallots, minced
6 leaves fresh basil, chopped
2 tablespoons chopped parsley
12 langoustine
20 raw clams, shucked
20 raw oysters, shucked
1 tablespoon virgin olive oil
12 medium shrimp, shelled and deveined
Pasta
Chopped parsley

Process butter, garlic, shallots, basil, and parsley until soft. The butter should be white in color. Sauté langoustine and shrimp in olive oil 3-4 minutes. Lower flame; add clams, oysters, and butter mixture. Melt butter slowly or it will separate. Add cooked fettuccine immediately; mix well and serve topped with chopped parsley.

FETTUCCINE PASTA
Flat Pasta Noodles ¼-inch wide

3¼ cups sifted flour
5 eggs
1 tablespoon olive oil
1 teaspoon salt
Olive oil
Salt

Mound flour on a board; scoop out center to form a well. Break eggs into a deep bowl, beat them with olive oil and salt; pour mixture into center of flour well. Working with fingers, mix flour into eggs a little at a time until it is incorporated; knead the mixture with both hands until it is quite firm and smooth to the touch. Dip a clean white cloth in warm water, wring out well, and wrap ball of dough in it to keep it from drying out. Set aside for 30 minutes. Roll dough into strips ¼ inch wide. Fill a 4-quart saucepan with 3 quarts of water. Add olive oil and salt. Bring to a boil; add fettuccine and stir. Do not let fettuccine stick together. Bring to a second boil for 2 minutes. Strain in a colander and pour cold water over pasta.

Chef Antonio Avona, Mario's Restaurant
Vaccaro Restaurants of Dallas

CIOPPINO
Serves 6

California's seafood stew

¼ cup chopped onion
¼ cup chopped Bell
  pepper (green)
2 cloves garlic, minced
⅓ cup olive oil
1 (1 lb., 13 oz.) can
  tomatoes
1 cup dry red wine
1 teaspoon marjoram
½ teaspoon thyme
1 bay leaf
1 teaspoon basil
3 tablespoons chopped
  parsley
2 teaspoons salt
¼ teaspoon pepper
3 pounds white fish, cut
  in slices
1 pound shrimp, peeled
  and cleaned
2 lobster tails, shelled and
  cut into bite-sized
  pieces
½ pound clams, minced
4 cups cooked rice or
  toasted Italian bread

Sauté onions, green pepper, and garlic in hot oil in large saucepan until tender. Add tomatoes, wine, marjoram, thyme, bay leaf, basil, and parsley. Cover; simmer 1 hour. Add salt, pepper, fish, shrimp, and lobster. Cook 20 minutes; do not stir. Add clams; cook 5 minutes. Remove from heat. Serve in bowls with toasted Italian bread or over hot rice.

Under Maestro Dorati, the activities of the orchestra expanded. So did its fame. In the late forties, the DSO was invited to participate on the national network series, "Orchestras of the Nation." Moreover, five albums were recorded and released by RCA Victor on its Red Seal label, to great acclaim.

CRABMEAT LORENZO   Serves 6

½ cup finely chopped
  green onion
1 cup finely chopped
  mushrooms
½ cup butter, melted
½ tablespoon Dijon
  mustard
½ cup dry white wine
1 cup thin white sauce
½ cup whipping cream
½ tablespoon
  worcestershire sauce
1 pound lump crabmeat
¼ cup finely chopped
  parsley
Salt
White pepper
4 pastry shells or
  artichoke bottoms

Sauté onions and mushrooms in butter until soft. Add mustard, wine, white sauce, cream, and worcestershire; heat. Add crabmeat and parsley; season with salt and white pepper; keep warm over hot water until served. Serve in pastry shells or on artichoke bottoms.

Miss Helen Corbitt

Substitute shrimp, mixed seafood or chicken.

FISH IN GREEN SAUCE   Serves 4
A dieter's delight

2 tablespoons lime juice
½ cup olive oil
1 small onion
1 teaspoon salt
5 cloves garlic, finely
  minced
½ cup finely chopped
  parsley
1 tablespoon vinegar
1 pound fish fillets

Preheat oven to 375°. Blend all ingredients except fillets until smooth. Arrange fish fillets in ovenproof dish. Pour sauce over fillets; cover and bake 30 minutes.

Dr. Francine Daner

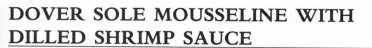

DOVER SOLE MOUSSELINE WITH
DILLED SHRIMP SAUCE

Serves 8

2 pounds sole or other
   white fish
4 egg whites
2½ cups whipping cream
Salt
White pepper
Red pepper
Butter
Parsley

Preheat oven to 375°. Process or grind fish fillets, adding egg whites one at a time. Purée again, pouring in cream slowly until mixture is completely smooth. Season to taste with salt, white pepper, and red pepper. Butter an 8-cup ring or charlotte mold. Pour in mousse; set in hot water bath. Cover mousse with a piece of buttered wax paper. Bake 25 minutes or until knife inserted comes out clean. Unmold and serve hot or cold with hot Shrimp Sauce.

Shrimp Sauce:
2-3 cups thick white
   sauce
¼ cup tomato juice
2 tablespoons dry sherry
2 tablespoons chopped
   fresh dill or 2
   teaspoons dried
   dillweed
Salt
Pepper
½ pound cooked shrimp,
   peeled and cleaned

Heat white sauce; stir in tomato juice. Flavor to taste with sherry, dill, salt, and pepper. Stir in shrimp.

Mrs. Joe M. Dealey, Jr. (Pam)

Center an elegant spring picnic on this mousse; toss in a baguette, crisp-cooked broccoli with Creamy Vinaigrette, Butternut Brie, chilled champagne, and fresh raspberries. Come to think of it, make this a very private picnic.

In 1949, the DSO offered its musical directorship to the brilliant associate conductor of the New York Philharmonic. After he accepted, Walter Hendl became at 32 the youngest conductor to head a major American orchestra. Hendl's seasons with the DSO sparkled with landmark performances, such as the 1952 DSO debut of a young student artist named Van Cliburn from Kilgore, Texas. The 1953-54 season saw the first dance soloist to perform with the Symphony. It was Martha Graham, who danced William Schuman's *Judith*.

FLOUNDER SUPREME WITH SHRIMP MOUSSE

Serves 8

Mousse:
1 pound raw shrimp, peeled
3 eggs
1 cup whipping cream
Salt
Pepper
Fresh parsley, chopped

Preheat oven to 350°. Purée shrimp; add 1 egg at a time, beating until absorbed. Add cream, salt, pepper, and parsley, blending thoroughly. Chill mixture.

Fish:
8 flounder fillets
Cognac
Salt
Pepper
Butter
1 cup dry white wine
¼ cup vermouth
¼ cup fish stock
¼ cup chopped shallots
Butter
Parchment paper

Sprinkle fillets with cognac, salt, and pepper. Place equal portions of shrimp mousse on fillets and roll into paupiettes. Place fish in buttered ovenproof dish; sprinkle with wine, vermouth, fish stock, and shallots. Cover with buttered parchment paper. Bake 10-15 minutes or until fish flakes.

Sauce:
Juice from baked fish
1 cup whipping cream
6-8 tablespoons butter, softened

In saucepan, cook juices from fish until reduced by half. Add cream and reduce again. Whisk in butter by the tablespoon. Serve sauce with fish.

Mrs. Tim Kirk (Jeannie)

For an all-star dinner, try Mushroom Flan as a first course, endive salad, Flounder Stuffed with Shrimp Mousse, and Soy-Glazed Snow Peas. Button up a perfect evening with Sorbet de Cassis and expresso.

OYSTERS BIENVILLE

Serves 6

New Orleans on the half shell!

1 cup finely chopped onion
½ cup butter, melted
½ cup flour
2 cups chicken broth, warmed
1½ pounds boiled shrimp, peeled and finely chopped
½ pound fresh mushrooms, chopped
3 egg yolks
½ cup half and half
½ cup white wine
1 teaspoon salt
1 teaspoon white pepper
½ teaspoon red pepper
Rock salt
3 dozen oysters on the half shell
¼ cup breadcrumbs
½ cup grated Parmesan cheese
⅛ teaspoon paprika

Preheat oven to 375º. Sauté onion in butter until tender. Slowly add flour, stirring constantly, until lightly browned. Add broth gradually, stirring constantly; simmer 10 minutes or until sauce is very thick. Stir in shrimp and mushrooms; cook 5 minutes and remove from heat. Whisk together egg yolks, half and half, and wine. Slowly pour small amount of warm sauce into egg mixture, stirring constantly to avoid curdling. Stir egg mixture into sauce; add salt, white pepper, and red pepper. Return to low heat, stirring constantly until very thick. Arrange layer of rock salt in bottom of 6 pie pans. Pour liquid from each oyster; place 6 oysters in shells in each pan. Bake 7 minutes. Remove from oven; increase temperature to 400º. Pour off excess liquid from oysters. Spoon sauce over each oyster. Combine breadcrumbs, cheese, and paprika; place on top of sauce. Return to oven; bake 10 minutes or until lightly browned. Serve immediately.

After his first concert at the beginning of the DSO's 59th season, Maestro Paul Kletski was called back to the stage for ten curtain calls and a standing ovation—a tribute last seen in Dallas when Sir Thomas Beecham conducted.

SPICY FILLET OF SOLE
Serves 4

4 fillets of sole
¾ cup flour
1 teaspoon salt
½ teaspoon pepper
½ teaspoon paprika
⅓ cup butter, melted
½ cup dry white wine
½ teaspoon ground
ginger
2 tablespoons lemon juice
2 tablespoons brown
sugar
2 bananas, quartered
lengthwise
4 tablespoons slivered
almonds, toasted

Use 1 large or 2 medium-sized saucepans to allow room for fillets or they will break. Mix flour, salt, pepper, and paprika. Dip fillets into mixture until thoroughly coated. Brown fillets in butter only 2-3 minutes on each side. Remove and keep warm. Add wine, ginger, lemon juice, and brown sugar to saucepan. Stir until sauce thickens slightly. Taste to correct seasonings. Add bananas; simmer 2 minutes. To serve, arrange bananas around fillets; strain hot sauce over fillets. Sprinkle with almonds.

Miss Helen Corbitt

For a mid-summer dinner, use Spicy Filet of Sole, quickly steamed green beans, Cucumber Mousse, and Avocado Cream.

SNAPPER WITH SHRIMP AND TOMATO MUSTARD SAUCE
Serves 8

3 pounds small fillets of
snapper
Salt
Pepper
½ pound small shrimp,
peeled and cleaned
1 cup chopped leeks
2 tablespoons butter,
melted
1 cup whipping cream
4 tablespoons tomato
paste
3 tablespoons Dijon
mustard
1½ teaspoons cornstarch

Preheat oven to 350°. Place snapper in a buttered 2-quart ovenproof dish. Sprinkle with salt and pepper. Spoon shrimp onto fillets. Sauté leeks in butter until limp; spoon over fish. Combine remaining ingredients; blend well; pour over leeks. Bake uncovered 30 minutes.

Fish may be prepared in advance and refrigerated. Allow fish to reach room temperature before baking.

VENETIAN SHRIMP

Serves 3-4

1 pound raw shrimp,
  peeled and cleaned
4 tablespoons butter,
  melted
2 teaspoons capers
4 tablespoons brandy
¾ cup whipping cream
1 tomato, peeled, seeded,
  and diced
2 teaspoons tomato paste
2 tablespoons cornstarch
Salt
Pepper
½-1 teaspoon tarragon
2-3 cups cooked rice

Sauté shrimp in butter just until shrimp turns bright pink. Add capers and brandy; ignite. Mix in cream, tomato, and tomato paste; heat until hot. Remove ½ liquid; mix in cornstarch. Return to shrimp mixture; stir until thickened. Add seasonings. Serve over rice.

Miss Helen Corbitt

For extra flash ladle this over Cream Cheese Soufflé instead of rice. Add Tangy Green Beans, homemade Party-Perfect Refrigerator Rolls, a simple tomato vinaigrette salad, and Orange Cream in Orange Cups. Look no further than Chicken Liver Pâté with Currants for an appetizer.

SHRIMP WITH WILD RICE

Serves 6-8

1 (6 oz.) package long
  grain and wild rice
  mix
¾ cup chopped onion
¾ cup chopped Bell
  pepper (green)
1 clove garlic, minced
½ teaspoon pepper
2-3 pounds shrimp,
  cooked, peeled, and
  cleaned
4 tablespoons butter,
  melted
¼ cup breadcrumbs
½ cup whipping cream
1 teaspoon worcestershire
  sauce

Preheat oven to 400°. Butter 2-quart ovenproof dish. Spread rice mixture on bottom; sprinkle onion, Bell pepper, and garlic on top. Add pepper. Arrange shrimp on top; dribble 2 tablespoons butter over shrimp. Add breadcrumbs and remaining butter. Mix cream and worcestershire together; pour over breadcrumbs. Cover with foil and bake 35 minutes.

Mrs. John E. Bromberg (Susan)

Do it ahead; bake it later.

LEMON FISH BROIL   Serves 4
(Lemon balm, parsley, dill)

4 cups fresh lemon balm
  leaves
2 pounds flounder fillets
4 tablespoons butter,
  melted
1 cup chopped fresh
  parsley
2 teaspoons fresh dill
Paprika
Salt
Pepper

Line buttered, ovenproof dish with
lemon balm leaves; spread fillets over
leaves. Blend butter, parsley, and dill
together; brush over top of fillets.
Sprinkle paprika over fillets and season as
desired. Broil 10 minutes; turn oven off;
cover and leave in oven for 15 minutes.

No-Salt Herb Blend:
Combine 4 tablespoons each oregano
leaves and onion powder (not onion
salt) with 4 teaspoons each marjoram,
basil, savory, garlic powder, thyme,
rosemary and 1 small amount at a time
in a mortar and pestle or in the
blender. Spoon into a salt shaker or
covered container. Makes about 1 cup.

Phyllis Shaudys

GRILLED SWORDFISH STEAK
WITH LEMON BUTTER   Serves 4

2 (1-1¼ lbs.) swordfish
  steaks, cut 1½-inches
  thick
4 tablespoons butter
¼ cup lemon juice
2 tablespoons anchovy
  paste
Salt
Pepper
Lemon wedges

Wipe swordfish steaks with damp paper
towel and pat dry. Combine butter,
lemon juice, anchovy paste, salt, and
pepper in small saucepan; heat. Place
steaks in ovenproof dish; spoon seasoned
butter over them. Broil 8-10 minutes
on each side, basting every 5 minutes.
Serve with lemon wedges.

BARBEQUE SHRIMP

Serves 4

2 pounds raw shrimp,
  unpeeled
¼ cup olive oil
Juice of 1 lemon
1 teaspoon hot pepper
  sauce
1 tablespoon
  worcestershire sauce
1 tablespoon red crushed
  pepper
1 teaspoon lemon pepper
  marinade
½ teaspoon oregano
¼ teaspoon basil
¼ teaspoon marjoram
1 teaspoon Italian herb
  seasoning
1 teaspoon seasoning salt
1 teaspoon celery salt
1 teaspoon thyme
3 cloves garlic, minced
½ cup chopped onion
½ cup chopped Bell
  pepper (green)
½ cup butter
¼ cup chopped parsley
1 lemon, thinly sliced

Preheat oven to 350⁰. Arrange shrimp in an ovenproof dish. Sprinkle each shrimp with all ingredients except butter, parsley, and lemon slices. Dot shrimp with butter, sprinkle with parsley, and garnish with lemon slices. Cover and bake 25 minutes or until shrimp turns pink. Drain sauce from shrimp and reserve in sauceboat.

Serve with a green salad, hot French bread, and lots of napkins.

When named Music Director of the Dallas Symphony Orchestra, Donald Johanos was one of only three American-born and trained musicians to head major American orchestras in 1962. He was no stranger to the DSO, having already served six seasons in Dallas as associate conductor and resident conductor. Among his many DSO triumphs: the Symphony's debut at Carnegie Hall in March, 1965.

CURRANT-GLAZED GAME HENS

Serves 4

6 slices bacon, cooked
  and crumbled
1 onion, chopped
1 Bell pepper (green),
  chopped
1 cup chopped celery
3 tablespoons butter
2 cups breadcrumbs
1 cup coarsely chopped
  nuts
1½ teaspoons thyme
½ teaspoon sage
1 egg, lightly beaten
1 cup chicken broth
4 Cornish game hens
½ cup butter, melted
½ cup dry white wine
1 clove garlic, minced
½ teaspoon salt
½ teaspoon sage
3 tablespoons flour
1 cup dry white wine
1 cup red currant jelly
1 teaspoon dry mustard
Salt

Preheat oven to 400°. Sauté bacon, onion, Bell pepper, and celery in butter until vegetables are soft. Add breadcrumbs, nuts, thyme, sage, egg, and broth; mix well. Stuff Cornish game hens and bake on a rack 1 hour 15 minutes. Combine butter, wine, garlic, salt, and sage; baste hens 5-6 times. Keep hens warm while preparing sauce. Drain pan juices into a saucepan; whisk in flour, wine, jelly, and dry mustard; bring to a boil, stirring constantly. Season to taste and serve over game hens.

Mrs. Addison Wilson (Susan)

Feast on Creamy Cauliflower Soup, game hens, Buffet Peas, muffins of Caramel Crusted Cranberry Bread and Frozen Pumpkin Bombe or Sweet Potato Pudding.

Georg Solti led the Dallas Symphony for one season as senior conductor. Solti was a giant in the music world — a conductor who had led many of the greatest orchestras, including the New York Philharmonic, the Vienna Philharmonic, the Paris Conservatoire, and the London Symphony. Never having been in Dallas, he agreed to a one-year contract after his stormy, long-distance resignation from the Los Angeles Philharmonic, and then became director of the Royal Opera, Covent Garden, London.

CHICKEN BREASTS HUNTER STYLE   Serves 6

6 (6-oz.) chicken breasts
⅓ cup flour
4 tablespoons butter,
    melted
½ cup brandy
2 cups sliced mushrooms
6 tablespoons finely
    chopped green onions
½ cup white wine
1 cup chicken broth
3 tablespoons chopped
    parsley
1 cup peeled, chopped
    tomato
Salt
Pepper

Flatten chicken breasts; salt and flour lightly and brown in butter. Add brandy and ignite. When flames die down, remove chicken and keep warm. In the same saucepan sauté mushrooms and green onions until transparent but not brown. Add wine; cook 1 minute, stir in broth, parsley and tomato. Simmer until slightly thickened. Add chicken breasts and rewarm 5 minutes. Season with salt and pepper. Serve hot over rice or noodles. Sprinkle with remaining 1 tablespoon parsley.

Miss Helen Corbitt

Gather the clan for this chicken dish served over brown rice, Zucchini Parmesan, and a warm fruit dessert like French Apple Tart.

WEINER BACKHENDL   Serves 4

4 chicken breasts,
    skinned and boned
¼ cup fresh lemon juice
Salt
½ cup flour
1 egg, lightly beaten
2 cups fresh breadcrumbs
Oil
Lemon wedges

Flatten chicken breasts and marinate several hours in lemon juice. Pat dry; salt on all sides and flour. Dip chicken pieces into egg; thoroughly coat with breadcrumbs. May be prepared several hours ahead to this point. Fry pieces in ¼-inch of hot oil until golden brown on both sides. Do not crowd pan. Keep completed pieces in warm oven, if necessary. Serve with lemon wedges.

In the spring think of this with asparagus spears, Vegetable Pâté, and Strawberries with Sherry Cream in stemmed glasses.

BAKED CHICKEN STRIPS
(Thyme and sweet basil)

Serves 8

7-8 boneless chicken breasts
2 cups fine breadcrumbs
1 cup Parmesan cheese
1½ teaspoons salt
1 teaspoon chopped fresh thyme
1 tablespoon chopped fresh sweet basil
1 cup butter, melted

Preheat oven to 400⁰. Cut chicken in 1½-inch strips. Combine breadcrumbs, Parmesan, salt, thyme, and basil. Dip chicken strips in butter and coat with crumbs. Place on lightly greased baking sheet. Bake 20 minutes, turning strips after 10 minutes.

Mrs. Bill Bogert (Mary)

The Solti season has become legendary for its electrifying performances. One evening, the audience cheered for 20 minutes after the performance of Beethoven's Fifth Symphony.

SOUTHERN FRIED CHICKEN

Serves 6-8

Shortening for deep fat frying
12-18 pieces chicken (thighs, breasts, and legs preferred)
4 cups self-rising flour
2 teaspoons salt
½ teaspoon pepper
2 cups buttermilk

Preheat shortening to 375⁰. Wash chicken, skin, and pat pieces dry. Stir together flour, salt, and pepper. Dip pieces into buttermilk and then flour. Fry pieces in shortening 12-15 minutes per batch, or until chicken is crispy and golden brown.

Mrs. Edwin R. DeYoung (Patti)

CHICKEN WOK

Serves 6

1½ cups cubed chicken
¼ cup oil
3 cups broccoli flowerets
1 Bell pepper (red), cubed
½ pound mushrooms, sliced
1 (10 oz.) can sliced water chestnuts
10 ounces snow peas
3 tablespoons chopped green onion
1 cup chicken broth
3 tablespoons dry sherry
2 tablespoons soy sauce
2 tablespoons cornstarch
½ teaspoon hot pepper sauce
1 teaspoon oyster sauce
4 cups cooked rice
Cashew nuts

In a wok, stir-fry chicken in hot oil 5 minutes and set aside. Add vegetables to wok; cook 3 minutes. Combine broth, sherry, soy sauce, cornstarch, hot pepper sauce, and oyster sauce; add to vegetables. Cook 5 minutes; add chicken and serve over rice. Top with cashew nuts.

Mrs. William C. McAfee (Louise)

Anshel Brusilow, former conductor of the Chamber Symphony of Philadelphia, was named resident conductor of the DSO for the 1970-71 season. Under Brusilow's baton, the Dallas Symphony made a determined effort to reach out for wider audiences. Maestro Brusilow led the orchestra in a series of "Dallasound" concerts that featured rock and popular compositions for full symphony orchestra.

GREEK CHICKEN WITH YOGURT   Serves 4

Lemony-tart and low in calories

1 whole chicken,
  quartered
1 lemon, sliced
Salt
Pepper
1 onion, chopped
4 tablespoons butter,
  melted
1 clove garlic, chopped
½ cup dry white wine
1 cup chicken broth
⅛ teaspoon nutmeg
1 (16 oz.) container plain
  yogurt
2 tablespoons flour
½ cup chicken broth
2 cups cooked rice

Rub chicken quarters with lemon, salt, and pepper. Sauté onion in butter; add chicken and brown. Add garlic, wine, broth, lemon slices, and nutmeg. Simmer 25 minutes or until chicken is tender. Remove chicken and keep warm while finishing sauce. Whisk yogurt and flour with pan juices; add up to ½ cup broth to make a thin sauce. Simmer, stirring occasionally, to reduce sauce by one quarter. Discard lemon slices and serve over rice.

CHINESE CHICKEN   Serves 4

Quick, crunchy, and wonderful

Sauce:
¼ cup honey
½ cup soy sauce
¼ cup red wine vinegar
1 clove garlic, minced
2 tablespoons sesame
  seed, toasted
⅛ teaspoon red pepper

Combine all ingredients.

4 cups cooked, shredded
  chicken
½-1 head iceberg lettuce,
  shredded
1 (3¾ oz.) package bean
  threads or 1½ cups
  bean sprouts
2 tablespoons oil
2-3 bunches scallions

Marinate chicken in sauce 30 minutes. Using wok or large saucepan, sauté bean threads in oil over high heat 1 minute; drain. Mix chicken, marinade, scallions, and lettuce with bean threads. Toss briefly over low heat to blend thoroughly. Serve immediately so that vegetables remain crisp.

Mr. Dan Clark

POULET HÉLÈNE

Serves 5-6

A creamy, elegant casserole

4 tablespoons butter
4 tablespoons flour
1½ cups hot milk
Salt
Pepper
1 tablespoon chopped green onion
1 tablespoon butter, melted
½ cup dry white wine or dry sherry
⅓ cup vermouth
1 teaspoon curry powder
¼ teaspoon worcestershire sauce
3 cups chopped cooked chicken
½ cup whole boiling onions, cooked
½ cup chopped artichoke hearts
½ cup mushrooms, halved or quartered
½-⅔ cup cooked green peas
½ cup breadcrumbs
¼ cup chopped parsley
3 tablespoons butter, melted
3 cups cooked noodles or 6 baked pastry ramekins

Preheat oven to 350°. Melt butter and add flour, stirring over medium heat a few minutes. Stirring constantly, whisk in milk and cook until white sauce thickens and bubbles. Season with salt and pepper; set aside. In medium saucepan sauté green onion in butter. Add wine, vermouth, curry powder, and worcestershire; cook 3 minutes. Stir in chicken, onions, artichoke hearts, mushrooms, green peas, and white sauce. Turn into greased, 1½-quart ovenproof dish. Sauté breadcrumbs and parsley in butter until crumbs are golden; use as topping. Bake 15-20 minutes or until brown and bubbly. Serve over noodles or in pastry.

Suzann Darrow

SPINACH AND CHICKEN CRÊPES   Serves 6

1 pound mushrooms,
  finely chopped
2 large onions, finely
  chopped
4 tablespoons butter,
  melted
2 pounds fresh spinach or
  2 (10 oz.) packages
  frozen spinach,
  cooked, well drained,
  and finely chopped
4 cups diced cooked
  chicken
½ cup sour cream
¼ cup dry sherry
1 teaspoon salt
⅛ teaspoon red pepper
24 crêpes
Sherry Cheese Sauce

Preheat oven to 350°. Sauté mushrooms and onions in butter until soft, and all liquid has evaporated. Add spinach, chicken, sour cream, sherry, salt, and red pepper. Put 1-2 tablespoons of filling on each crêpe and roll. Arrange in a buttered, shallow ovenproof dish. Spoon sauce over crêpes and bake 30-45 minutes until sauce is bubbling and lightly browned.

Filled crêpes may be refrigerated or frozen. When ready to bake, defrost; pour sauce over and bake as directed.

Crêpes:
4 eggs
2 cups milk
4 tablespoons butter,
  melted and cooled
  slightly
1 teaspoon salt
¼ teaspoon nutmeg
1 cup sifted flour
Butter

Yields 24 (6 - 7-inch) crêpes. Combine eggs, milk, butter, salt, nutmeg, and flour; blend until smooth. Refrigerate 2 hours. Heat crêpe pan or shallow saucepan and brush lightly with butter. Ladle in approximately 2 tablespoons batter and quickly tilt pan to spread batter evenly; pour out any excess batter. Cook until lightly browned, approximately 1 minute, then turn and cook until browned on other side.

Crêpes may be made in advance, stacked with wax paper between every 3-4 and refrigerated or frozen.

(continued on next page)

Sherry Cheese Sauce:
4 tablespoons butter, melted
½ cup flour
4 cups chicken broth
2 cups milk
1 cup grated Parmesan or Swiss cheese
1 cup dry sherry
Salt
Red Pepper

Yields 6 cups

Combine butter and flour; cook gently 2 minutes. Blend in broth and milk; cook over low heat, stirring until smooth and thickened. Add cheese, sherry, salt, and red pepper. Stir until cheese is melted.

SWISS CHICKEN   Serves 6

6 boneless chicken breasts
Salt
Pepper
2 eggs, lightly beaten
1 cup breadcrumbs
4 tablespoons oil
4 tablespoons butter
¼ cup flour
1¼ cups milk
1 teaspoon salt
1 teaspoon pepper
1¼ cups dry white wine
1 cup grated Swiss cheese
Tomato
Avocado

Pound chicken to ¼-inch thickness. Season with salt and pepper. Dip in egg; roll in crumbs to coat. Heat oil in saucepan; brown chicken approximately 2 minutes on each side. Brown in 2 batches; clean out saucepan and add new oil for second batch; set aside. In another saucepan, melt butter; add flour; stir until blended. Add milk; stir until thick. Season with salt and pepper. Remove from heat; add wine. Pour half of sauce in bottom of 9x13-inch ovenproof dish. Arrange chicken pieces in single layer. Pour remainder of sauce over chicken. Chill several hours or overnight. Preheat oven to 350°. Bake, covered, 50 minutes; uncover. Sprinkle with cheese. Garnish with slices of tomato and avocado. Return to oven 2 minutes.

Mrs. Harry J. McBrierty (Vikki)

STUFFED PHEASANT WITH ORANGE SAUCE

Pheasant
Butter
Salt

Preheat oven to 350°. Rub cavity of pheasant with butter and salt.

Stuffing:
Pheasant giblets, chopped
1 teaspoon salt
4 cups water
1 cup wild rice
2 tablespoons chopped
onion
1 tablespoon chopped
Bell pepper (green)
¼ cup chopped celery
4 tablespoons butter,
melted
1 strip bacon

Drop giblets into boiling salted water; simmer 15 minutes and remove. Stir in rice and cook until almost tender. Sauté onion, Bell pepper, and celery in butter 3 minutes. Add drained rice and giblets; stir and spoon into pheasant cavity. Lay bacon over breast; bake 15-20 minutes per pound. Remove bacon last 15 minutes of cooking.

Sauce:
3 tablespoons butter
4 tablespoons flour
1⅓ cups chicken broth
¼ teaspoon salt
¼ teaspoon paprika
1 tablespoon grated
orange rind
⅔ cup orange juice,
heated
2 tablespoons sherry
Raisins (optional)

Melt butter and stir in flour until brown. Slowly add broth; season with salt and paprika. Keep sauce warm in double boiler over low heat. Just before serving add rind, orange juice, sherry, and raisins.

Miss Carla Coldwell

Pheasant may also be prepared with cornbread dressing or no dressing at all. Add onion, orange slice, and apple if no stuffing is used.

RABBIT IN SALSA VERDE
Serves 8

2 rabbits, cut into serving
    pieces
Olive oil
6 stalks celery, chopped
1 large onion, chopped
1 fresh hot green chili,
    chopped or 2-3
    jalapeño chilies,
    chopped
40 cloves garlic, peeled
Salt
Pepper
½ cup dry white wine
2 cups chopped fresh
    tomatillos
2 tablespoons butter
1 (8 oz.) container plain
    yogurt
Coriander or Italian
    parsley, chopped

Preheat oven to 350°. Dip rabbit in oil, coating all sides. Make bed of celery, onion, and chilies in bottom of heavy, deep saucepan. Arrange rabbit pieces on top, tucking garlic cloves in among them; sprinkle with salt and pepper. Pour wine over; bring to a simmer on top of stove; cover with foil and lid to prevent steam from escaping. Cook 1 hour in oven. Test to see if meat is tender. Sauté tomatillos in butter; combine and heat thoroughly. Remove rabbit pieces to serving platter and keep warm. Purée contents of saucepan to make a smooth paste. Add yogurt and blend until smooth. Skim off fat if necessary. Return sauce to saucepan and heat thoroughly, being careful not to boil. Correct seasonings. Pour sauce over rabbit and sprinkle with coriander or parsley.

For South-of-the Border gourmet, add Cauliflower-Chili Soufflé, Avocado and Carrot Salad, and flan or an orange dessert.

ELK BACKSTRAP WITH ONION AND GREEN PEPPER RINGS

Serves 6-8

2-3 pounds elk backstrap, sliced ¼-inch thick or elk steaks
¾ cup flour
¼ cup olive oil
2 onions, sliced in rings
Salt
Pepper
2 teaspoons mixed herbs
2½ cups beef, chicken, or game broth
2 tablespoons worcestershire sauce
2 teaspoons hot pepper sauce
4 Bell peppers (green), sliced into rings
½ cup red wine

Dust elk with flour. Brown in hot oil. Add onions, seasonings, broth, worcestershire, and hot pepper sauce. Cover and simmer 1 hour. Add Bell pepper and wine. Simmer uncovered 30 minutes.

Mrs. R.C. Wynn (Melinda)

Venison may also be used.

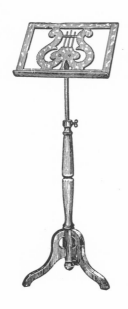

A native Texas, Louis Lane, was invited to join the DSO in 1973 as principal guest conductor; he became the orchestra's artistic advisor in 1974. A brilliant man and gifted musician, Lane conducted the DSO with dignity and with a flair for performance. His tenure as artistic advisor was marked by both highs and lows in the life of the Symphony. In 1974, he led the orchestra through one of its most difficult times, when a lack of funds forced a temporary suspension of activities. He was also on the podium the following year for the DSO's triumphant 75th anniversary.

SCALLOPINI OF VENISON

Serves 4-6

Marinade:
1 quart milk
2 cloves garlic, minced
¼ teaspoon salt
¼ teaspoon pepper

1½ pounds venison,
  sliced and pounded
  thin
1 onion, chopped
2 tablespoons butter,
  melted
½ pound fresh
  mushrooms, sliced
1 (14½ oz.) can beef
  broth
1 tablespoon
  worcestershire sauce
1 tablespoon soy sauce
⅛ teaspoon hot pepper
  sauce
1 teaspoon bead molasses
1 cup flour
4 tablespoons butter
¼ cup oil
½ cup Marsala wine

Combine milk, garlic, salt, and pepper; mix well. Marinate meat 2 hours. Sauté onion in butter until brown. Add mushrooms; cook 4-5 minutes. Add broth, worcestershire, soy sauce, hot pepper sauce, and molasses. Stir and simmer 15 minutes. Remove meat from marinade. Dredge meat in flour and fry in butter and oil approximately 30 seconds on each side. Add meat and wine to mushroom mixture. Simmer 30 minutes. Serve with rice.

A blue-and-white striped circus tent housed the popular Summertop series at NorthPark from 1975-1978. Summertop featured the DSO and some of the biggest "pop" stars. In 1979, the series was rechristened Starfest and moved to the more spacious and bucolic setting of the lawn at Electronic Data Systems. Starfest moved to Park Central in 1982.

BEEF MADEIRA   Serves 6-8

2 tablespoons butter,
  melted
1 tablespoon oil
3-4 pounds beef
  tenderloin
2 tablespoons butter
1 onion, finely chopped
½ cup finely chopped
  carrots
½ cup finely chopped
  celery
1 leek, finely chopped
¾ cup beef consommé
¾ cup chicken broth
1 cup Madeira
Parsley
1 bay leaf
⅛ teaspoon thyme
Salt
Pepper
1 teaspoon arrowroot

Preheat oven to 375°. In ovenproof dish combine butter and oil; brown tenderloin on all sides and remove from pan. Add butter and all vegetables to drippings; sauté until vegetables soften. Place browned beef over vegetable mixture; stir in consommé, chicken broth, Madeira, a few sprigs of parsley, bay leaf, thyme, salt, and pepper. Bring to boil; insert meat thermometer in center of roast; cover and bake in oven until temperature registers 140°. Remove meat; degrease pan juices, discarding parsley and bay leaf. Boil liquid until reduced to ⅓ of its original volume. In separate bowl add small amount of sauce to arrowroot and stir to dissolve. Whisk into sauce and cook until slightly thickened. Season to taste; serve over sliced tenderloin.

Miss Helen Corbitt

BLEU CHEESE FLANK STEAK   Serves 4

3 pounds flank steak
½ pound mushrooms,
  sliced
2 tablespoons butter
3 tablespoons crumbled
  bleu cheese
1 clove garlic, minced
Salt
Pepper

Cut a pocket in steak. Sauté mushrooms in 1 tablespoon butter. Add remaining butter, cheese, garlic, salt, and pepper; cool. Stuff into pocket. Close with skewers and broil 3 inches from coals to desired doneness.

Mrs. David A. Nelson (Elaine)

BEEF WITH MUSTARD SAUCE   Serves 4

½ pound mushrooms,
  sliced
½ cup minced onion
1 tablespoon butter,
  melted
1 pound round steak, cut
  in thin strips
½ teaspoon salt
½ teaspoon pepper
1 teaspoon paprika
1 cup thin white sauce
½ cup dry vermouth
1 tablespoon Dijon
  mustard
½ cup sour cream
Buttered noodles

Sauté mushrooms and onions in butter until limp. Add steak and sauté 5 minutes. Combine salt, pepper, paprika, white sauce, and vermouth. Stir into onion and meat mixture; simmer 5 minutes. Combine mustard and sour cream; stir into saucepan. Serve with buttered noodles.

BEEF TENDERLOIN
STUFFED WITH MUSHROOMS   Serves 12

4-5 pounds beef
  tenderloin
4 tablespoons butter
1 pound mushrooms,
  chopped
½ cup chopped celery
½ cup chopped onion
¼ cup chopped Bell
  pepper (green)
1 teaspoon salt
½ teaspoon pepper
¼ teaspoon sage
¼ teaspoon thyme
2 tablespoons flour
Parsley

Preheat oven to 325°. Starting at widest end of tenderloin, slit meat down middle and spread apart. Sauté mushrooms in butter until liquid evaporates; add celery, onion, Bell pepper, salt, pepper, sage, and thyme. Sauté until vegetables are tender. Blend in flour; cook 1 minute. Stuff mixture into pocket of beef. Secure opening with skewers; lace with string. Roast 20 minutes per pound for medium rare. Garnish with parsley.

WINE-SAUCED BEEF TENDERLOIN   Serves 10

4½-5 pounds beef
   tenderloin
3 tablespoons butter
2 cloves garlic, sliced in
   half
3 tablespoons
   worcestershire sauce
¼ cup red wine
¼ cup red wine and
   garlic vinegar
½ pound mushrooms,
   sliced
6 tablespoons butter
Salt
Pepper
Chopped parsley

Preheat oven to 400°. Rub beef with butter, garlic, and worcestershire. Bake uncovered on a rack in an ovenproof dish 30-35 minutes or until thermometer reaches 130°-140°, rare in middle, medium on ends. Remove from oven. Drain juices into saucepan. Rinse ovenproof dish with wine and vinegar; add to saucepan. Wrap beef in foil until serving time; do not refrigerate. This may be done 2-3 hours in advance. At serving time sauté mushrooms in butter 2 minutes; add juices. Heat beef in foil 10 minutes or until hot. Remove beef to platter; season with salt, pepper, and parsley. Combine extra juice from foil with mushroom mixture; heat. Place sauce in serving dish.

Mrs. Hardy E. Thompson, III
(Susan)

Impress red meat lovers with the flavor of Wine-Sauced Beef Tenderloin, Spinach-Filled Turnips, baked potatoes, and Chocolate Marble Cheesecake.

BURGUNDY BEEF BROCHETTE
Serves 4

Seasoning salt
Pepper
1½ pounds sirloin, cut in
   1½-inch cubes
½ cup burgundy
1 teaspoon worcestershire
   sauce
1 clove garlic
½ cup oil
2 tablespoons ketchup
1 teaspoon sugar
½ teaspoon salt
1 tablespoon vinegar
½ teaspoon marjoram
½ teaspoon rosemary
12 large mushrooms
3 Bell peppers (green),
   quartered
12 boiling onions
3 apples, halved and
   seeded

Sprinkle seasoning salt and pepper over sirloin and refrigerate about 3 hours. In large mixing bowl, combine burgundy, worcestershire, garlic, oil, ketchup, sugar, salt, vinegar, marjoram, and rosemary. Add sirloin and marinate in refrigerator about 3 more hours. Alternate sirloin, mushrooms, Bell peppers, onions, and apples on skewers; cook over charcoal fire, basting with remaining marinade.

Ms. Sheryn R. Jones

STEAK DIANE
Serves 6

6 (6 oz.) filet mignon
4 tablespoons butter
2 tablespoons salad oil
1 clove garlic, minced
3 shallots, minced
4 tablespoons brandy
2 tablespoons butter
¼ teaspoon tarragon
3 tablespoons chili sauce
½ cup brown sauce*

Pound steaks to ½-inch thickness. Pan broil in butter and oil; remove from pan. Add garlic and shallots; cook over low heat. Add brandy, stand back and ignite. (Always have a lid or baking sheet nearby to control the flame.) Remove from heat and whisk in butter, tarragon, chili sauce, and brown sauce.

To make a quick brown sauce, mix ½ cup bouillon, ½ teaspoon Kitchen Bouquet, 2 teaspoons worcestershire, 1 teaspoon minced onion, and 1 teaspoon ketchup; boil for 5 minutes.

GREEN CHILI FLANK STEAK   Serves 4

1 flank steak
Salt
Pepper
6 tablespoons butter
1 (4 oz.) can chopped
  green chilies, drained
1-2 jalapeños, chopped
  (optional)
2-3 cloves garlic,
  chopped

Pound flank steak until uniformly flat. Salt and pepper to taste. Process butter, garlic, and chilies into a smooth paste; spread over steak. Roll lengthwise and skewer or toothpick closed. Refrigerate several hours. Shape bowl of heavy-duty foil to fit steak roll; grill **rare** over charcoal. Slice into thin round slices, serving chili butter with each portion.

Mrs. W. Dwight Calkins (Linda)

Make believers out of gringos with Green Chili Flank Steak, Super Spanish Rice, mountains of tortillas, guacamole or Picado Dip, and Mango Mousse.

STEAK AU POIVRE   Serves 6

4 tablespoons crushed
  black peppercorns
6 (6 oz.) tenderloin
  steaks, pounded
2 tablespoons olive oil
2 tablespoons butter
3 tablespoons brandy
½ cup minced shallots
¾ cup dry white wine
1 cup whipping cream
1 tablespoon Dijon
  mustard
½ teaspoon tarragon
2 tablespoons chopped
  parsley

Press crushed peppercorns into steaks. Heat oil and butter in heavy saucepan; add steaks and sauté 3-4 minutes on each side for medium rare. Pour brandy over pan and ignite; when flames die, remove steaks and keep warm. Cook shallots in same saucepan until translucent, using an additional tablespoon of butter if necessary to keep shallots from sticking. Whisk in wine and bring to a boil; add cream and boil again. Add mustard and tarragon; reduce liquid by ⅓ and pour over steaks. Garnish with parsley.

Try Steak au Poivre with grated carrots sauteed with parsley and butter, Pommes Byron, and Fresh Orange Cake layered with whipped cream and strawberries.

SOUTHWESTERN CHALUPAS

Serves 8

1 pound pinto beans
2 teaspoons salt
1 large onion, chopped
2 cloves garlic, diced
1 (4 oz.) can green
chilies
1 cup taco sauce
1 (14½ oz.) can whole
tomatoes, chopped
½ teaspoon oregano
½ teaspoon cumin seed
½ teaspoon pepper
1 pound ground beef
1 onion, chopped
12 (6-inch) tostados

Toppings:
Shredded lettuce
Grated cheese
Chopped tomatoes
Chopped onions
Chopped black olives
Sour cream
Jalapeños
Picante sauce
Guacamole

Soak pinto beans in cold water overnight. Drain; cover with 2 inches water. Add salt and simmer 1 hour, adding water if needed. Add onions, garlic, chilies, taco sauce, tomatoes, oregano, cumin seed, and pepper. Simmer 1-1½ hours or until beans are tender. Brown ground beef with onion; stir into beans. To serve, ladle portion of beans and meat over each tostado and layer toppings to taste.

The Dallas Symphony Orchestra League Cooking School uncovered its first pot in March of 1963. Exotic foods and familiar dishes were both among the specialties presented by Helen Corbitt at the Cooking School, held at Neiman-Marcus's Zodiac Room.

SHANGHAI SKEWERED STEAK

Serves 4

1 pound flank steak
3 tablespoons light soy sauce
3 tablespoons dark soy sauce
2 tablespoons sugar
4 tablespoons sherry
2 cloves garlic, minced
4 tablespoons fresh ginger, minced
4 tablespoons sesame oil

Cut steak into ¼-inch slices across the grain. Combine remaining ingredients and use to form marinade. Marinate steak several hours or overnight. Prior to cooking, string beef strips onto bamboo skewers; grill. Cook only a few minutes on each side.

Mr. Nelson Spencer

For an Oriental evening, try Chinese Vegetable Soup, Egg Rolls, Shanghai Skewered Steak over rice, and Peking Almond Cream.

SWEDISH POT ROAST

Serves 8

4 pounds beef rump roast
1 teaspoon salt
1 teaspoon allspice
½ teaspoon pepper
3 tablespoons butter
2 onions, sliced
½ cup beef broth
1½ teaspoons anchovy paste
2 bay leaves
2 tablespoons vinegar
2 tablespoons molasses
2 tablespoons cornstarch, blended with 2 tablespoons water
1 cup sour cream
½ teaspoon anchovy paste

Rub beef on all sides with salt, allspice, and pepper. Heat butter in 5-quart baking dish; add beef and brown on all sides. Add onions; brown. Stir in broth, anchovy paste, bay leaves, vinegar, and molasses; cover and simmer 2½ hours. Remove beef to serving plate. Blend cornstarch mixture into sour cream. Add to dish; stirring. Add anchovy paste. Stir until thickened. Serve with roast.

Mrs. William M. Pederson (Patt)

Serve with French Stuffed Cabbage for a real treat.

SOUTH SEA BEEF

Serves 12

4 pounds beef, cut in
  1-inch cubes
½ cup salad oil
2 (20 oz.) cans pineapple
  chunks
3 tablespoons soy sauce
2 tablespoons vinegar
2 cups diced celery
2 cucumbers, sliced
2 tomatoes, peeled and
  cut in wedges
2 Bell peppers (green),
  cut in 1-inch squares
2 onions, thinly sliced
4 teaspoons cornstarch
4 tablespoons water
6 cups cooked rice

Brown beef in oil. Drain pineapple; add syrup to saucepan with soy sauce and vinegar. Bring to boil; simmer 15 minutes. Add pineapple and vegetables; cook 5 minutes. Combine cornstarch and water; gradually add to beef mixture, stirring constantly until thickened. To serve, spoon rice around edge of platter; turn beef mixture into center.

Mrs. Kenneth Bardin, Jr. (Melinda)

VEAL CUTLET PROVENÇAL

2 pounds veal steak
Salt
Pepper
½ cup flour
½ cup olive oil
2 cloves garlic, finely
  chopped
2 tomatoes, peeled,
  seeded, and finely
  chopped
½ cup red wine
2 tablespoons chopped
  fresh parsley
12 ripe olives

Season veal steak; dredge with flour. Sauté slowly in olive oil; brown on both sides. Add garlic; cover; simmer 10 minutes over low heat. Add tomatoes and red wine; cover; simmer until tender. Add parsley and ripe olives; remove from heat. Mix sauce well; pour over steak. Serve with white or wild rice.

Mrs. Norman P. Ross (Jean)

CREAMY VEAL
AND WATER CHESTNUTS
Serves 6-8

Full-flavored company favorite

3 pounds boneless veal, cubed
4 tablespoons butter, melted
1 large onion, chopped
2 cloves garlic, minced
Salt
Pepper
⅛ teaspoon red pepper
1 pound mushrooms, quartered
4 tablespoons butter, melted
1½ cups beef broth
¼ teaspoon nutmeg
¼ teaspoon thyme
1 bay leaf
1 (8 oz.) can sliced water chestnuts, drained
½ cup whipping cream
2 egg yolks, beaten
2 tablespoons lemon juice
Fresh parsley, chopped

Preheat oven to 375°. Brown veal in butter; add onion and garlic; sauté until soft. Season with salt, pepper, and red pepper. Place in 3-quart, ovenproof dish. Sauté mushrooms in butter; place in ovenproof dish. Deglaze saucepan with broth. Add remaining broth to saucepan; add nutmeg, thyme, bay leaf, and water chestnuts. Pour over veal and mix well; may be refrigerated at this point. Cover and bake 1 hour 30 minutes. Combine cream, egg yolks, and lemon juice. Add to veal mixture; stir and bake uncovered 15 minutes. Sprinkle with parsley.

In 1966, the Ford Foundation offered a $2.5 million grant to the DSO, if the orchestra could raise matching funds. A similar offer went to other orchestras across the country. Ralph B. Rogers, President of the Dallas Symphony Association, led the Symphony's fund-raising effort. In June of 1967, Dallas became the first orchestra to announce that it had successfully met the Ford challenge.

ESCALOPES DE VEAU MADAGASCAR   Serves 4

Gorgeous...

1½ pounds veal scallops
½ cup flour
¾ cup clarified butter,
   melted
3 ounces brandy
1½ teaspoons chopped
   shallots
30 green peppercorns
1 tablespoon Dijon
   mustard
1¼ cups reduced veal
   stock or beef bouillon
¾ cup whipping cream
Salt
White pepper
Papaya and/or
   strawberries
Watercress

Lightly dust veal with flour; sauté in butter over high heat 2 minutes for each side. Remove to platter and keep warm. Discard butter; remove saucepan from heat. Add brandy, shallots, peppercorns, and mustard to saucepan; stir well. Add stock and return to heat; bring to boil. Add cream, salt, and pepper. Reduce heat; stir until sauce is dark tan in color, approximately 3 minutes. Garnish with slices of papaya and/or strawberry fanned on both sides of plate with watercress on top.

LEMON VEAL WITH SCALLIONS   Serves 4

1 pound veal scallops
Salt
Freshly ground pepper
1 tablespoon olive oil
2 tablespoons butter
8 paper-thin lemon slices
4 scallions, chopped
1 sprig fresh tarragon or
   rosemary
2 tablespoons chopped
   parsley
2 tablespoons butter
4 tablespoons dry white
   wine

Season veal with salt and pepper. Heat oil and butter in saucepan; when it froths, add pieces of veal, lemon, scallions, and herbs. Cook veal 1 minute on each side until done, but juicy. Transfer veal mixture to dish; keep warm. Add remaining butter to pan with wine and heat gently, scraping surface of pan with wooden spoon. Pour pan juices over veal and serve.

Complete your menu with Spinach-Yogurt Dip, Zucchini with Parmesan, and Blueberry Soufflé.

VEAL PAUPIETTES WITH CHICKEN MOUSSELINE

Serves 8

½ pound chicken, boned
1 egg
1¼ cup whipping cream
1 tablespoon salt
1½ teaspoons white pepper
⅛ teaspoon nutmeg
16 large veal scallops
16 slices bacon
¼ cup brandy
1 cup white wine
¼ cup green peppercorns, rinsed and drained
2 cups whipping cream or 1 cup whipping cream and ½ cup veal stock

Purée chicken until smooth; add egg and blend. Slowly add cream and seasonings until completely absorbed. Refrigerate 2 hours. Place a heaping tablespoon of chicken stuffing on each veal scallop and roll into paupiettes. Roll bacon around each paupiette and secure with toothpick. Brown veal in skillet and drain bacon drippings from pan. Add brandy and wine; cook covered 10 minutes. Add green peppercorns and cream; simmer. Place veal paupiettes on serving dish and pour sauce over each.

Mrs. Tim Kirk (Jeannie)

Stuff your best hunting buddies into black tie, light the candles, and present Veal Paupiette over wild rice, Bibb lettuce tossed with a light vinaigrette and toasted walnuts, Carrot Terrine, and Pears in White Wine.

Mitch Miller donated his services as conductor of the DSO at a Sing-A-Long concert in April, 1975. The event raised funds for Symphony musicians.

VEAL FONESTIER
Serves 4

1½ pounds veal chops,
  thinly sliced
2 cloves garlic
1 cup flour
4 tablespoons butter,
  melted
½ pound mushrooms,
  thinly sliced
Salt
Pepper
⅓ cup dry vermouth
1 teaspoon lemon juice
Parsley

Rub veal with garlic. Dip in flour, coating each side thoroughly. Sauté veal in butter until golden brown. Heap mushrooms on top of veal. Sprinkle with salt, pepper, and vermouth; cover and cook over low heat 20 minutes or until tender. Keep veal moist. Add a tablespoon of water or vermouth if necessary. Before serving sprinkle with lemon juice and parsley.

Mrs. James B. Scott (Janet)

Collect compliments with Brie Soup, this irresistible veal, Spinach Mornay in Tomatoes, and Dacquoise au Chocolat.

BAKED HAM WITH CUMBERLAND SAUCE
Serves 10

5-8 pounds precooked
  ham

Heat ham according to instructions.

Cumberland Sauce:
3 tablespoons red currant
  jelly
2 tablespoons port
2 tablespoons orange
  juice
1 tablespoon lemon juice
1 teaspoon dry mustard
½ teaspoon ginger
1 teaspoon paprika
3 tablespoons finely
  grated orange rind

Melt jelly over low heat; combine with remaining ingredients. Pour over ham to serve.

Head straight for the deep South when you plan ham, Rich Squash Casserole, buttery steamed spinach, and Royal Chess Pie. Squeeze in time to make Grandma's Biscuits, they're worth it.

HAM LOAF WITH RAISIN SAUCE
AND MUSTARD MOLD

Serves 12

Especially for fall luncheons

3½ cups ground cooked
    ham
8 ounces ground veal
8 ounces ground round
2 cups day-old bread,
    broken in large chunks
¼ teaspoon poultry
    seasoning
½ teaspoon salt
¼ teaspoon pepper
1 egg, beaten
1 onion, finely chopped
¼ cup chopped parsley
¼ cup ketchup
2 celery stalks, finely
    chopped
¾ cup milk
½ cup packed brown
    sugar

Preheat oven to 350⁰. Combine all
ingredients and mix well. Bake 1 hour
in loaf pans. May be frozen, defrosted,
and baked.

Raisin Sauce:
1 cup packed brown
    sugar
2 teaspoons cornstarch
¼ cup vinegar
¼ cup lemon juice
½ teaspoon lemon peel
1 cup water
1 cup raisins
¼ cup dry sherry

Yields 3 cups
Mix sugar and cornstarch. Slowly add
remaining ingredients and cook over
low heat. If sauce is not thick enough,
remove some liquid and add 1 teaspoon
cornstarch, mixing well; cook until
thickened.

(Continued on next page)

Mustard Mold:

Serves 10-12

4 eggs, beaten
½ cup vinegar
½ cup sugar
1 tablespoon dry mustard
1 teaspoon tumeric
Salt
1 envelope unflavored
  gelatin
¼ cup water
1 cup whipping cream,
  whipped

Combine eggs and vinegar in double boiler; mix well. Add sugar, mustard, tumeric, and salt; cook. Dissolve gelatin in water; add to sauce; cool. Fold in cream; turn into individual molds or a 1-quart mold.

Mrs. Barton Darrow (Ann)

SAUSAGE MUSHROOM STRUDEL

Serves 10

1 pound Italian sausage
1 pound mushrooms,
  finely chopped
1 tablespoon chopped
  shallots
1 (8 oz.) package cream
  cheese, softened
8 frozen strudel sheets
1 cup butter, melted
¾ cup dry breadcrumbs
3 tablespoons butter,
  melted

Preheat oven to 400°. Fry sausage in large saucepan; crumble and remove from pan. Pat dry. Drain all but 2 tablespoons of drippings. Add mushrooms and shallots to pan and sauté until all liquid is evaporated. Return sausage to pan; stir in cream cheese and cool. Using 4 strudel sheets for each roll, unfold 1 sheet, brush with butter and sprinkle with breadcrumbs. Repeat with second and third sheets; top with fourth sheet. Spoon half of mixture along long side of sheets. Tuck short ends toward center to keep filling intact; roll like a jelly roll. Place roll on buttered baking sheets and brush with butter. Bake 20 minutes.

Mrs. Kenneth Bardin, Jr. (Melinda)

This freezes well, but must be thawed thoroughly before baking.

CARIBBEAN ROAST PORK

Serves 10-12

5-6 pound pork loin roast
1 cup packed brown
  sugar
¼ cup dark rum
1 tablespoon finely
  chopped garlic
2 teaspoons ginger
½ teaspoon cloves
¾ teaspoon oregano
1 bay leaf, crumbled
1 teaspoon salt
¼ teaspoon pepper
2 cups chicken broth
2 teaspoons cornstarch
¼ cup rum
3 tablespoons lime juice

Score the fat side of pork roast at 1-inch intervals. Combine brown sugar, rum, garlic, ginger, cloves, oregano, bay leaf, salt, and pepper; rub well into all sides of roast. Cover and refrigerate overnight. Preheat oven to 350⁰. Roast meat on rack until interior temperature registers 160⁰-165⁰, approximately 30 minutes per pound. Keep pork hot while preparing sauce. Bring pan juices to a boil. Stir chicken broth and cornstarch together; whisk into pan juices; cook and stir until lightly thickened and reduced by one-fourth. Add rum and lime juice. Season to taste and serve over sliced pork.

Leftovers make wonderful tacos or burritos; shred meat and reheat.

Have a planter's party with Cuban Black Bean Soup, Caribbean Roast Pork, Gingered Papayas, and Mango Mousse. Drink lots of rum, smoke fine cigars, and plot revolution.

The Junior Group of the Dallas Symphony Orchestra League organized Symphony YES (Youth Education Services) in 1975 to further educate Dallas school children about the Symphony Orchestra.

PEABODY HOTEL STUFFED ONIONS   Serves 6

6 large onions
1 clove garlic, minced
1 tablespoon butter, melted
1 cup ground ham
1 (10 oz.) package frozen chopped spinach, cooked and drained
3 cups cooked rice
1 cup breadcrumbs
1 egg, beaten
1 cup chicken broth
Salt
Pepper
1/8-1/4 teaspoon sage
3/4 cup grated Parmesan cheese
3/4 cup breadcrumbs
4 tablespoons butter, melted

Preheat oven to 400°. Cut onions in half and carefully remove centers, leaving shell about 1/4-inch thick. Boil shells until tender; chop remaining onion and sauté with garlic in butter until tender. Combine chopped onion, and garlic with ham, spinach, and rice; stir in breadcrumbs and egg. Moisten with chicken broth and season with salt, pepper, and sage. Fill onion shells; mix cheese and breadcrumbs to sprinkle over top. Brush with butter and bake until brown on top.

Mrs. G. Mallory Willis (Martha)

Ground beef, chicken or turkey may be substituted for ham.

SWEET AND SOUR PORK   Serves 4

4 center-cut pork chops
2 tablespoons oil
3/4 cup minced onion
1 clove garlic, minced
1 1/2 teaspoons cornstarch
1 cup pineapple juice
2 tablespoons vinegar
1 tablespoon soy sauce
1 teaspoon brown sugar
1/4 teaspoon curry powder
1/8 teaspoon pepper
3 strips lemon peel
2 tablespoons tomato juice

Preheat oven to 350°. Brown chops in oil on both sides. Place in ovenproof dish in which they will lay flat. Pour off all but 2 tablespoons fat in saucepan; add onions and garlic. Sprinkle with cornstarch and stir in remainder of ingredients; mix well. Stirring constantly over low, heat 5 minutes. Pour sauce over chops; cover and bake 1 hour or until chops are done.

LAMB CURRY

4 tablespoons curry powder
½ teaspoon ginger
½ teaspoon tumeric
¼ teaspoon paprika
¼ teaspoon red pepper
½ teaspoon salt
¼ teaspoon pepper
2½ pounds boned lamb shoulder, cut in bite-sized cubes
6 tablespoons butter, melted
2 onions, chopped
2 stalks celery, chopped
1 Bell pepper (green), chopped
1 clove garlic, minced
2 tart apples, cored and chopped
½ cup raisins
2 tablespoons flour
1 cup chicken broth
2 cups coconut milk
4 tablespoons chutney
6-8 tablespoons yogurt
4 cups cooked rice

Combine spices; set aside. Sauté lamb in butter until brown. Remove meat; sauté onions, celery, Bell pepper, and garlic in same saucepan. While cooking, add half of spice mixture. When vegetables are tender, add apples and raisins. Sprinkle with flour; add broth and coconut milk. Add remaining spice mixture and browned lamb; simmer 15 minutes. Blend in chutney and yogurt. Serve on rice.

A richly flavored curry that's not burning hot.

ROAST LAMB, GREEK STYLE   Serves 8

Salt
Pepper
2 eggplants, peeled and
   thinly sliced
2 tablespoons olive oil
2 onions, chopped
2 cloves garlic, minced
2 tablespoons chopped
   fresh mint or 2
   teaspoons dried mint
2 tablespoons chopped
   parsley
2 tablespoons olive oil
4-5 pound lamb roast,
   boned
Salt
Pepper
½ cup white wine
⅓ cup olive oil
Juice of 1 lemon
1 teaspoon oregano
1 cup white wine
Salt
Pepper

Heavily salt and pepper eggplants; brown on both sides in oil; set aside. Lightly brown onions, garlic, mint, and parsley in oil. Spread onion mixture over lamb; salt and pepper; arrange eggplant on top. Roll and tie lamb. Place on rack in ovenproof dish; pour wine over meat. Allow to rest several hours or overnight. Brown lamb at 450° 15 minutes; reduce heat to 300°; cook approximately 2 hours. Combine oil, lemon juice, and oregano. Baste meat frequently. When lamb is cooked; set aside. Skim grease from saucepan juices; simmer several minutes with wine, salt, and pepper; serve as sauce for lamb.

Plan to serve with a clear soup, tossed green beans and snow peas, lemon-buttered rice, and Cold Apricot Soufflé with Apricot Sauce.

HERBED LAMB CHOPS

(Basil, rosemary, garlic, mint)

3 teaspoons chopped
   fresh basil
3 teaspoons chopped
   fresh rosemary
1 clove garlic, minced
1 teaspoon chopped fresh
   mint
1 teaspoon salt
6 lamb chops
Juice of ½ lemon
3 tablespoons salad oil

Combine herbs and seasonings; spread mixture on large plate and place chops on top. Leave 1 hour, turning a couple of times, to absorb herb flavors. Place chops under oven broiler and cook about 6 minutes on each side basting with oil and lemon juice while cooking.

Mrs. J. J. Hastings

111

MOROCCAN LAMB

Serves 4

3 pounds lamb shoulder, cut in 2-inch cubes
4 tablespoons oil
6 ounces mushrooms, sliced
1 onion, chopped
½ cup raisins
½ cup blanched almonds
3 tablespoons sugar
2 teaspoons cinnamon
1 teaspoon cloves
1 teaspoon allspice
1 teaspoon salt
1 (16 oz.) can tomatoes

Brown lamb on all sides in oil. Remove from pan. Drain off all but 2 tablespoons of oil. Add mushrooms and onions; cook until lightly browned. Stir in raisins, almonds, sugar, and seasonings; simmer 5 minutes. Add browned lamb and tomatoes. Simmer, covered 1½ hours. Serve over hot rice.

Flee to the Casbah with Moroccan Lamb, Lahvash, and Oranges Orientale.

RISOTTO RUSTICA

Serves 8

Turns a company dinner into a festival

Rice:
2 onions, chopped
3 cloves garlic, chopped
3 tablespoons olive oil
2 cups rice
Zest of 1 lemon
Juice of 1 lemon
2 teaspoons tarragon
2 teaspoons salt
Pepper
3½ cups chicken broth
1 cup vermouth

Sauté onions and garlic in oil. Add rice, lemon zest and juice, seasonings, broth, and vermouth. Simmer 20-25 minutes until rice is done. Season to taste.

Lemon Marinade for Shrimp or Veal:
1 pound shrimp, peeled and cleaned, or 1 pound veal scallopini, cut in ½-inch strips

Combine shrimp or veal and garlic, salt, pepper, oil, and lemon juice. Marinate overnight. Grill or sauté in marinade over high heat 3-4 minutes.

(continued on next page)

2-3 cloves garlic,
  chopped
1 teaspoon salt
½ teaspoon pepper
4 tablespoons oil
2 tablespoons lemon juice

**Oregano Marinade for
  Chicken:**
1 pound chicken breast,
  cut crosswise into
  ½-inch strips
1 clove garlic, chopped
1 teaspoon dried oregano
1 teaspoon salt
½ teaspoon pepper
4 tablespoons oil
1 tablespoon vinegar
1 pound Italian sausage
  (in casings) or ham,
  cubed
1 pound fresh spinach,
  cooked and squeezed
  dry or 1 (10 oz.)
  package frozen
  spinach, thawed and
  squeezed dry

Garnish:
1½ cups green peas,
  cooked or 1 (10 oz.)
  package frozen green
  peas, thawed
1 cup garbanzos, cooked
2-4 tomatoes, coarsely
  chopped
1 bunch cilantro,
  chopped

Prepare chicken using Oregano
Marinade. Bake Italian sausage or ham
until done. Cut sausage into ¼-inch
rounds. Toss rice with spinach; arrange
on a serving platter. Place meats in
concentric circles over rice and garnish
with peas, garbanzos, tomatoes, and
cilantro.

Mrs. Richard L. Collier (Leslie)

*Dish may be partially prepared ahead
by pre-cooking meats and preparing
garnish. Before serving, cook rice; toss
with meats to rewarm; arrange on
platter and top with garnish. A
combination of any 3 meats may be
used.*

*This one-dish spectacular may be
prefaced with antipasto and
accompanied only by crisp-cooked
broccoli in Creamy Vinaigrette and
Italian bread. For dessert try Cassata
alla Siciliana or White Magic Mousse.*

MANICOTTI
Serves 12-15

Easy to do for a crowd

5 pounds Italian sausage
5 (28 oz.) cans whole
tomatoes
5 onions, chopped
5 cloves garlic, chopped
5 (4 oz.) cans tomato
paste
5 teaspoons oregano
4 teaspoons basil
Salt
Pepper
2 pounds ricotta cheese
10 ounces Mozzarella
cheese, grated
½ cup grated Parmesan
cheese
2 eggs, lightly beaten
¾ teaspoon salt
⅛ teaspoon white pepper
¼ cup chopped parsley
28-30 crêpes

Preheat oven to 200°. Brown sausage; drain. Chop tomatoes, reserving juice. Combine sausage, tomatoes, and their juices, onions, garlic, tomato paste, oregano, and basil; cover and bake 6-8 hours or overnight. Season to taste. Turn oven to 350°. Combine cheeses, eggs, salt, pepper, and parsley. Fill crêpes with 2-3 tablespoons mixture and place in greased ovenproof dish. Cover crêpes with meat sauce; bake 30 minutes or until it bubbles.

Mrs. William R. Peeler (Kittye)

Ground beef may be substituted for half of the Italian sausage. Manicotti freezes well if meat sauce and crêpes are frozen separately. Thaw before assembling and baking.

When Voice of America taped a subscription concert during the DSO's 1975 season, it was estimated that 50,000,000 people around the world heard the broadcast.

SPAGHETTI PRIMAVERA   Serves 6-8

2 tomatoes, sliced
2 tablespoons olive oil
4 cloves garlic, chopped
¼ cup chopped parsley
Salt
Pepper
15 mushrooms, sliced
4 cloves garlic, chopped
4 tablespoons olive oil
1 cup sliced zucchini,
    blanched
1½ cups chopped
    broccoli, blanched
1½ cups snow peas,
    blanched
1 cup green peas
6 asparagus stalks, sliced
1 pound spaghetti,
    cooked al dente
¾ cup grated Parmesan
    cheese
⅓ cup butter, melted
1 cup whipping cream,
    warmed
⅓ cup chopped fresh
    basil
Salt
Pepper
⅓ cup pine nuts
    (optional)
Whole cherry tomatoes

Sauté tomatoes in oil with garlic, parsley, salt, and pepper. In another saucepan, lightly sauté mushrooms and garlic in oil; stir in zucchini, broccoli, snow peas, and asparagus just to heat vegetables. Toss spaghetti with cheese, butter, cream, basil, salt, and pepper. Top with vegetables, pine nuts, and sautéed tomatoes. Garnish with whole cherry tomatoes.

Mrs. R. C. Wynn (Melinda)

LINGUINE WITH ZUCCHINI AND PESTO SAUCE
Serves 4

(Basil)

Pesto Sauce:
2 cups fresh basil leaves
2 cloves garlic
½ cup pine nuts
½ cup grated Parmesan
¼ cup olive oil
½ teaspoon salt
½ teaspoon pepper

Pesto Sauce:
Purée all ingredients. Refrigerate. Best if made a day in advance. Sauce freezes well.

Linguine:
2 - 3 zucchini, cut into
  1-inch sticks
4 tablespoons butter,
  melted
¼ cup pine nuts
1 (1 lb.) package
  linguine, cooked al
  dente
Parmesan cheese

Linguine:
Sauté zucchini sticks in butter and add pine nuts. Mix hot linguine, zucchini, and pesto sauce together; sprinkle generously with Parmesan cheese.

SPAGHETTINI WITH SHRIMP AND MUSHROOMS
Serves 2

Luscious and buttery

1 clove garlic, minced
¾ cup sliced mushrooms
½ cup butter, melted
½ pound raw shrimp,
  peeled and cleaned
4 ounces thin spaghetti,
  cooked al dente
3 tablespoons grated
  Romano or Parmesan
  cheese
½ teaspoon salt
Pepper
Grated Romano cheese

In a large saucepan sauté garlic and mushrooms in butter. Add shrimp; cook 5 minutes. Add spaghetti. Sprinkle with cheese and seasonings. Using large spoon carefully turn spaghetti over from the edge of saucepan to center. Continue until spaghetti is very hot; do not let butter brown. Place on warm serving dish and serve with Romano cheese.

Mrs. Thomas S. Palmer (Margo)

116

ZUCCHINI AND MUSHROOM FETTUCCINE

Serves 8

½ pound mushrooms, thinly sliced
4 tablespoons butter, melted
1½ pounds zucchini, julienned
1 cup whipping cream
½ cup butter
¾ cup grated Parmesan cheese
½ cup chopped fresh parsley
8 ounces fettuccine, cooked al dente
Grated Parmesan cheese

In large saucepan, sauté mushrooms in butter over moderate heat 2 minutes. Add zucchini, cream, and butter; simmer 3 minutes. Add cheese and parsley to zucchini mixture. Toss well with fettuccine and serve immediately with additional Parmesan cheese.

Mrs. Allen E. Cullum (Sissy)

SPINACH RICOTTA TART

Serves 6-8

3 tablespoons butter, melted
1 small onion, finely chopped
1 pound spinach or 1 (10 oz.) package frozen spinach, cooked and squeezed dry
½ teaspoon salt
¼ teaspoon nutmeg
⅛ teaspoon pepper
½ cup Ricotta cheese or ¼ cup freshly grated Parmesan cheese
1 cup half and half
3 eggs, well beaten
1 (9-inch) pie shell, unbaked

Preheat oven to 350°. Sauté butter and onions; add spinach, salt, nutmeg, and pepper. In separate dish combine cheese, half and half, and eggs; stir into spinach mixture, mixing well. Pour into unbaked pie shells and bake 50 minutes.

ROQUEFORT AND ONION PIE

Serves 6-8

1½ cups flour
½ cup butter
1 egg yolk
2½-3 tablespoons cold
   water
½ teaspoon salt
4 large onions, sliced
Salt
Pepper
⅛ teaspoon thyme
2 tablespoons butter,
   melted
7 ounces Roquefort
   cheese, crumbled
2 eggs
4 egg yolks
½ cup milk
1½ cups whipping cream
Salt
Pepper
Nutmeg
1 (9-inch) pie shell,
   unbaked

Preheat oven to 400°. Combine flour, butter, egg yolk, water, and salt and chill dough for 30 minutes. Line buttered pie pan with chilled dough that has been rolled out; chill until firm. Line dough with wax paper pressing it into edges. Fill with pie weights or uncooked beans and bake 10-12 minutes until pastry begins to brown. Remove paper and weights; bake 3-5 minutes until bottom is no longer soft. Remove from oven and cool slightly. Lower oven to 375°. Sauté onion, salt, pepper and thyme. Place piece of buttered foil on top and cover with lid. Cook over low heat 20-30 minutes until onions are soft, stirring occasionally. Stir in Roquefort cheese until melted. Remove smooth mixture from heat and cool slightly; spread in pie shell. Beat eggs and egg yolks thoroughly with milk, cream, salt, pepper and nutmeg to taste.

Add filling to pie shell, filling ¾ full and bake 15 minutes. When mixture is partially set, add remaining custard to fill pie shell. Bake 25-30 minutes or until browned. Serve hot or at room temperature.

Anne Willan

HAM AND CHEESE SANDWICHES   Serves 8

4 tablespoons butter
¼ cup mustard
1 teaspoon poppy seeds
¼ cup grated onion
8 slices Swiss cheese
8 slices ham
8 Kaiser rolls or
    hamburger buns

Preheat oven to 300°. Process all
ingredients and spread on rolls. Wrap
in foil and bake 20 minutes.

Mrs. John K. Smith (Shirley)

Add horseradish to taste.

PARSLEY
SANDWICHES   Yields 42 finger-sized sandwiches
(Curly parsley and garlic chives)

1 pound bacon, fried
    crisp and crumbled
1 large bunch parsley,
    chopped with scissors
Mayonnaise
1 (1 lb.) loaf of thin
    white bread
Garlic-chive seasoned
    butter

Combine bacon and parsley with
enough mayonnaise to make a spread.
On each slice of bread, spread garlic-
chive butter, then bacon-parsley
mixture. Put 2 slices together to make
a sandwich. Return all sandwiches to
bread wrapper and refrigerate or freeze.
To serve, slice each sandwich into 3
finger-sized sandwiches or 6 bite-size
sandwiches. Thaw covered with barely
damp cloth.

Mrs. I. J. Newton (Mary)

Sandwich Fillings:

Roll cooked asparagus tips in thin slices of buttered bread.

Combine chopped canned mushrooms and black olives with mayonnaise and serve on open-face sandwich piled high in center.

Mix sautéed fresh mushrooms with Roquefort or bleu cheese and serve on whole wheat bread.

Mix crabmeat or shrimp with celery and cucumber, celery and pineapple, celery, avocado, and tomato.

Mix cream cheese and chopped candied or preserved ginger with buttered bread.

Mix soft Cheddar cheese with green chilies.

Mix chopped chicken, celery, and almonds with mayonnaise and season with chicken soup mix.

Mix liverwurst and cream cheese, season with a little sherry wine, on rye bread.

Combine thin sliced baked ham with thinly sliced apples sprinkled with cinnamon and mustard flavored butter.

Be sure to use thin bread for better sandwiches and fewer calories. Season butter with soup mixes, lemon juice, or juices from roasts. Make open-face for a change.

Miss Helen Corbitt

Vegetables

ARTICHOKES ITALIAN

Serves 6-8

2 (10 oz.) packages
   frozen artichoke
   hearts, cooked
4 tablespoons butter,
   melted
Grated Parmesan cheese
4 slices bacon, cubed
1 onion, minced
½ cup wine
1 (6 oz.) can tomato
   paste
1 teaspoon oregano
1½ teaspoons salt
¼ teaspoon pepper
1 teaspoon sugar
Grated Parmesan cheese

Lightly sauté artichoke hearts in butter; arrange in ovenproof dish and sprinkle with Parmesan cheese. In another saucepan sauté bacon and onion until golden. Add wine, tomato paste, and seasonings. Pour sauce over artichokes; brown under broiler. Top with additional Parmesan cheese.

Mrs. James B. Scott (Janet)

GREAT GREEN BEANS

Serves 6

2 cups diagonally sliced
   celery
2 tablespoons butter,
   melted
1 tablespoon cornstarch
¾ cup chicken broth
2-3 tablespoons soy sauce
2 teaspoons sesame seeds,
   toasted
¼-½ teaspoon garlic salt
2 pounds cut green
   beans, cooked
1 (8 oz.) can sliced water
   chestnuts, drained

Sauté celery in butter until tender. Combine cornstarch, broth, soy sauce, sesame seeds, and garlic salt; add to celery mixture and cook stirring constantly until mixture thickens. Add green beans and water chestnuts and heat thoroughly.

Mrs. John F. Lehman, Jr. (Linda)

TANGY GREEN BEANS
Serves 8

A go with everything vegetable

2 tablespoons Dijon
  mustard
1 tablespoon sugar
⅓ cup butter
2 tablespoons lemon juice
2 tablespoons vinegar
Salt
Pepper
2 pounds green beans,
  cooked and drained

In saucepan combine mustard, sugar, butter, and salt. Simmer and stir in lemon juice and vinegar. Pour over green beans and heat well.

Mrs. G. Myrph Foote, Jr. (Sila)

FRENCH STUFFED CABBAGE
Serves 8

1 (1½-2 lb.) head
  cabbage
½ cup chopped onions
4 teaspoons butter,
  melted
¼ cup fine breadcrumbs
1 teaspoon salt
½ teaspoon white pepper
¼ teaspoon nutmeg
3 tablespoons chopped
  parsley
2 eggs, lightly beaten
Salt
½ cup butter
2 tablespoons lemon juice

Remove outer leaves from cabbage and wash thoroughly. Peel 10-12 whole leaves from cabbage by cutting them loose at the bottom. Line a 2-quart bowl with a cloth at least 12-inches square and place cabbage leaves, stems up, overlapping in bowl to form cup. Remove core from cabbage and discard. Sauté cabbage and onion in butter until limp; do not brown. Put cabbage and onion into bowl; add breadcrumbs, salt, pepper, nutmeg, parsley, and eggs, stirring quickly to mix. Stuff cabbage mixture into cabbage-lined bowl and twist cloth tightly closed. Tie a strip around the top and drop into boiling salted water. Simmer uncovered 1 hour, turning once. Melt butter and add lemon juice. To serve drain cabbage mixture and place in bowl; top with lemon butter.

MEXICAN CORN CASSEROLE
Serves 4-6

½ cup butter
1 (8 oz.) package cream
cheese
2 (12 oz.) cans shoepeg
corn, drained
1 (4 oz.) can chopped
green chilies
1 tablespoon sugar
Salt
Pepper
2 tablespoons butter

Preheat oven to 350⁰. Melt butter and cream cheese over low heat. Add corn, chilies, and spices. Pour in a buttered ovenproof dish and bake for 30 minutes.

Joni Owen

CARROT TERRINE
Serves 12-24

Famous for a very good reason

2 pounds carrots, peeled
and very thinly sliced
4 tablespoons butter
Salt
Pepper
5 eggs
2 extra egg yolks
1 tablespoon orange
flower water

Preheat oven to 450⁰. Place sliced carrots in large saucepan with water to cover. Add butter, salt, and pepper. Steam, stirring frequently, until tender enough to cut with fork. Do not overcook. Drain carrots, reserving liquid. Set carrots aside; return liquid to saucepan. Cook until reduced to ½ cup. Cool. Beat eggs, egg yolks, and orange flower water. Stir in carrot liquid. Fold in carrots, blending well. Spoon into well-buttered 9x5x3-inch glass ovenproof baking dish. Mixture should be very juicy. Cover dish with aluminum foil. Place dish in hot water bath. Bake 1 hour 15 minutes, or until puffed on top. Let stand at room temperature 15-20 minutes. Turn out, slice, and serve.

L'Ambiance Restaurant

Orange flower water may be purchased at specialty food stores.

CARROT PURÉE

Serves 4-6

1½ pounds carrots,
  peeled, cooked, and
  drained
1 tablespoon butter,
  melted
1 teaspoon sugar
Salt
Pepper
4 tablespoons whipping
  cream

Purée carrots. In saucepan combine butter and carrots; heat thoroughly. Add sugar, salt, and pepper. Beat in cream gradually. Taste for seasonings. Purée may be made 6-8 hours in advance and reheated. Keep covered at room temperature. To serve, place in a bowl and mark top in waves with a knife.

Anne Willan

Substitute 2 tablespoons sherry for half of the cream as a special twist.

CAULIFLOWER-CHILI SOUFFLÉ

Serves 6-8

¼ cup finely chopped
  onion
1 tablespoon butter,
  melted
2 pounds cauliflower,
  cooked and puréed
¼ cup wheat germ
¼ cup half and half or
  milk
4 egg yolks, beaten
1 (4 oz.) can chopped
  green chilies
½ teaspoon salt
4 egg whites, stiffly
  beaten
2 tablespoons butter
Wheat germ
½ cup grated Cheddar
  cheese

Preheat oven to 350°. Sauté onion in butter. Mix cauliflower, onions, wheat germ, half and half, egg yolks, chilies, and salt. Fold in egg whites. Pour mixture into a buttered 2-quart ovenproof dish. Sprinkle with wheat germ and top with cheese. Bake 30 minutes.

Suzann Darrow

CREAM CHEESE SOUFFLÉ
Serves 4-6

Instead of rice or potatoes

4 eggs, separated
⅛ teaspoon salt
1 teaspoon flour
¼ teaspoon mustard
⅛ teaspoon red pepper
2 (3 oz.) packages cream
   cheese, softened
1 cup sour cream

Preheat oven to 300°. Beat egg yolks until thick and creamy. Add salt, flour, mustard, and red pepper. Combine cream cheese and sour cream; blend until smooth; add to egg yolks and beat until smooth. Beat egg whites until stiff but not dry; fold into yolk mixture. Place in ungreased 1½-quart soufflé dish. Place in hot water bath and bake 1 hour.

Miss Helen Corbitt

Use as dessert soufflé with fruit sauce. If using as dessert, omit mustard and red pepper and add ¼ cup sugar.

EGGPLANT AND MUSHROOM CASSEROLE
Serves 8-10

2 pounds eggplant,
   peeled and cubed
1 tablespoon salt
1 cup chopped onion
1 pound mushrooms,
   chopped
6 tablespoons butter,
   melted
3 eggs, beaten
⅔ cup mayonnaise
1 (3 oz.) package cream
   cheese, softened
¼ cup chopped parsley
⅛ teaspoon thyme
3 tablespoons grated
   Gruyère cheese
¼ cup breadcrumbs
Butter

Preheat oven to 350°. Cover eggplant with water; add salt and set aside 30 minutes. Drain and cook in water until tender; drain again and cut into cubes. Sauté onion and mushrooms in butter until soft; add to eggplant. Stir in eggs and mayonnaise; mix thoroughly. Pour into buttered 2-quart ovenproof dish. Combine cream cheese, parsley, thyme, cheese, and breadcrumbs; sprinkle over eggplant mixture. Dot butter over top. Bake 30-40 minutes or until set and top is brown.

Miss Helen Corbitt

May be made ahead and refrigerated until ready to heat and serve.

EGGPLANT SOUFFLÉ
Serves 6

1 medium eggplant,
  peeled and cubed
2 eggs, separated
1 cup medium white
  sauce, using evaporated
  milk
1 cup grated Cheddar
  cheese
1 teaspoon onion juice
Salt
Pepper

Preheat oven to 375°. Parboil eggplant until tender; drain and mash. Beat egg whites until stiff. Fold egg whites and remaining ingredients into eggplant. Pour into greased ovenproof dish and set in pan of hot water. Bake 30 minutes or until brown.

Mrs. C. E. Willis (Mary)

FRESH BROCCOLI GRATINÉE
Serves 6-8

2 pounds broccoli or 3
  (10 oz.) packages
  frozen broccoli spears
Butter
Salt
Pepper
3 cups white sauce
2 ounces mild Cheddar
  cheese, grated
⅓ cup sliced almonds
2 tablespoons chopped
  pimiento

Preheat oven to 350°. Separate broccoli spears into serving size portions; cook and drain. Place in buttered ovenproof dish in single layer with heads overlapping stems. Sprinkle with salt and pepper. Pour white sauce over broccoli. Place half of grated cheese on top of sauce. Sprinkle sliced almonds over this and cover with remaining cheese. Arrange pimiento pieces as final decoration. Bake until cheese has melted and sauce is bubbly.

Mrs. Oscar W. Ponder (Evelyn)

BRAISED LEEKS IN CREAM
Serves 6

Fantastic company dish

8 large leeks
8 slices bacon, cut in
   2-inch pieces
1 cup water
Salt
Pepper
⅛ teaspoon thyme
2 tablespoons butter
2 tablespoons flour
1 cup milk
1 egg yolk
½ cup whipping cream
2 tablespoons grated
   Swiss cheese

Trim leeks, cutting off root ends and all but 2 inches of light green. Cut stalks in half lengthwise and wash thoroughly holding leaves apart. Again, cut in half lengthwise, then into 2-inch pieces. Brown bacon in saucepan; drain trimmings. Add leeks, water, salt, pepper, and thyme. Cover and cook until leeks are tender and water has evaporated, approximately 20-25 minutes. Make white sauce with butter, flour, and milk. Combine egg yolk and cream; whisk into hot sauce. Place leeks in a buttered ovenproof dish and top with sauce. Sprinkle with cheese; bake 20 minutes or until golden.

MUSHROOM FLAN
Serves 8

2 tablespoons chopped
   shallots
½ cup butter, melted
2 pounds mushrooms,
   coarsley chopped
Juice of ½ lemon
¼ cup Madeira or dry
   sherry
1 tablespoon flour
1 teaspoon salt
½ teaspoon white pepper
2 cups whipping cream
9-inch pie shell, baked
2 tablespoons chopped
   parsley
¼ cup grated Parmesan
   cheese

Preheat oven to 350°. Sauté shallots in butter until limp, but not brown. Add mushrooms and lemon juice; cook until almost dry. Add Madeira and cook until it evaporates. Stir in flour, salt, and pepper; add cream and cook until sauce thickens. Pour into baked pie shell and sprinkle with parsley and cheese. Bake 15 minutes.

Let it shine alone as a first course.

129

GINGERED PAPAYAS

Serves 8

4 firm, ripe papayas
½ cup butter
¼ cup lime juice
1 teaspoon ginger
8 thin slices lime
Red pepper

Preheat oven to 350°. Cut papayas in half, lengthwise, and scoop out seeds. Arrange in ovenproof dish with ⅛-inch warm water in bottom. Melt butter with lime juice and ginger. Pour butter mixture into papaya halves. Bake 30 minutes, basting 10 minutes before done. Garnish each papaya half with a slice of lime. Sprinkle with red pepper and serve warm.

BUFFET PEAS

Serves 6

2 tablespoons butter
1 (10 oz.) package frozen
   peas
2 cups shredded lettuce
¼ cup chopped onion
1 teaspoon salt
¼ teaspoon pepper

Combine butter and peas in large saucepan. Cover and cook slowly until peas are thawed completely. Add lettuce, onion, and seasonings, mixing lightly. Cover tightly and steam 4 minutes; serve immediately.

Mrs. John F. Lehman, Jr. (Linda)

SOY-GLAZED SNOW PEAS

Serves 6-8

1½ pounds snow peas
2 tablespoons butter,
   melted
2 tablespoons soy sauce
Juice of ½ lemon
Pepper

Cut each snow pea diagonally into 3 pieces. Add to butter; stir-fry 1 minute. Make a well in center of peas; add soy sauce and lemon juice; simmer a few seconds; toss with peas. Cook, stirring until snow peas are tender-crisp.

MUSHROOM MOUSSE

Serves 10-12

2 pounds mushrooms,
  finely chopped
4 cups whipping cream
Salt
Pepper
5 shallots
⅛ teaspoon nutmeg
10 eggs
5 egg yolks

Preheat oven to 350°. Process all ingredients to smooth consistency. Reserve 1 cup to serve as sauce. Pour into greased ovenproof dish. Set dish into larger pan containing hot water. Bake 20 minutes or until knife inserted in center comes out clean. Whisk reserved sauce over moderate heat until slightly thickened and spoon over each serving.

Mrs. Harry J. McBrierty (Vikki)

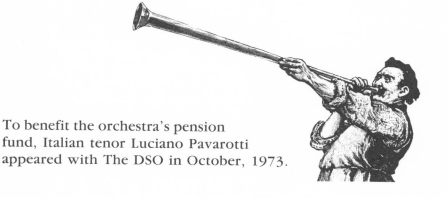

To benefit the orchestra's pension fund, Italian tenor Luciano Pavarotti appeared with The DSO in October, 1973.

NOODLES IN VERMOUTH

Serves 3-4

½ cup chopped onion
2 tablespoons butter,
  melted
2 cups curled macaroni
  noodles
¼ cup vermouth
2 cups chicken broth
¼ cup chopped Bell
  pepper (green)
Chopped ham (optional)

Sauté onion in butter. Add noodles, vermouth, and chicken broth. Cook over medium heat stirring constantly, approximately 20 minutes. This is good served as a side dish or as a main dish with ham and Bell pepper added.

Mr. Lon Orenstein

GOURMET POTATOES Serves 8-10

½ cup chopped onion
½ cup chopped Bell
 pepper (green)
4 tablespoons butter
2 cups grated Cheddar
 cheese
1½ cups sour cream
½ cup chopped pimiento
1 teaspoon salt
¼ teaspoon pepper
6 cups cooked and
 coarsely shredded
 potatoes
¼ teaspoon paprika

Sauté onion and Bell pepper in butter until limp; add cheese and stir until melted. Remove from heat and combine sour cream, onion, Bell pepper, pimiento, salt, pepper, and potatoes. Place in greased 9 x 13-inch ovenproof dish. Refrigerate overnight. Top with paprika, bake at 350° 30 minutes.

Potatoes may be prepared in advance and refrigerated overnight before baking.

POMMES BYRON Serves 6-8

4 potatoes, baked
1 cup grated Gruyère
 cheese
½ cup butter
1 teaspoon salt
½ teaspoon white pepper
⅛ teaspoon nutmeg
½-¾ cup whipping
 cream
½ cup Gruyère cheese

Preheat oven to 350°. Scoop potato out of shells; place in large bowl. Mix cheese, butter, salt, pepper, nutmeg, and cream with potatoes. Fill potato shells and place in a greased ovenproof dish. Bake 30-40 minutes. Sprinkle with ½ cup cheese and broil until brown.

Mrs. Leslie D. Scott (Onita)

COGNAC RICE
Serves 4-6

½ cup golden raisins
½ cup cognac or other brandy
1 onion, chopped
3 tablespoons butter, melted
1 cup rice
2½ cups chicken broth
½ cup shelled pistachios
2 tablespoons minced parsley
Salt
Pepper

Soak raisins in cognac 1 hour. Sauté onions in butter and add raisins and cognac. Stir in rice and brown slightly. Add broth; bring to a boil and simmer 25 minutes or until rice is done. Fluff and toss with pistachios and parsley. Season to taste.

Mrs. Kent Densing (Barbara)

Perfect with roasted Cornish Game Hens, a crisp green vegetable, Capered Asparagus Salad, light dinner rolls, and Chocolate Velvet.

SUPER SPANISH RICE
Serves 6

1 large onion, chopped
1 small Bell pepper (green), chopped
2 tablespoons butter, melted or bacon drippings
1 cup brown rice
2½ cups chicken or beef broth
¼ cup tomato sauce
½ teaspoon salt
1 teaspoon cumin
1 cup cooked garbanzos
1 large tomato, chopped and seeded
2-3 tablespoons cilantro, chopped

Sauté onion and Bell pepper in butter; add rice and brown lightly. Stir in broth, tomato sauce, and seasonings; simmer until rice is tender, approximately 50 minutes. Stir in garbanzos, tomato, and cilantro; heat thoroughly before serving.

Mrs. Kipp Murray (Gwen)

RABATON   Serves 5

1 (10 oz.) package frozen
   spinach, cooked and
   squeezed dry
5 ounces ricotta cheese
¼ cup grated Parmesan
⅔ cup breadcrumbs
2 eggs
1 clove garlic, chopped
Salt
¼ cup flour
5 cups chicken broth
½ cup butter
½ teaspoon sage

Preheat oven to 350°. Combine spinach, ricotta cheese, Parmesan, breadcrumbs, eggs, garlic, and salt. Form into small sausage shapes about 2 inches long. Bring broth to a boil. Roll sausages in flour and drop them carefully into boiling broth. Boil no more than 20 sausages at a time. Sausages will float to the top in a short time. Continue to boil for another 2-3 minutes. Lift them from broth with a slotted spoon and place them in an oiled ovenproof dish. Melt butter and pour over Rabaton. Sprinkle with sage and bake 10 minutes.

Suzann Darrow

HERB RICE   Serves 10
(Garlic, bay, marjoram, basil, thyme)

3 tablespoons minced
   onion
1 tablespoon minced fresh
   garlic
4 tablespoons butter,
   melted
2 cups uncooked rice
2 bay leaves
1 teaspoon fresh marjoram
½ teaspoon fresh basil
1 teaspoon fresh thyme
4 cups chicken broth

Sauté onions and garlic in butter, but do not brown. Add rice, bay leaves, marjoram, basil and thyme; cook until translucent. Pour in hot broth and simmer 25 minutes.

Absolutely wonderful!

SPINACH SOUFFLÉ RING WITH MUSHROOMS
AND ONION IN SOUR CREAM   Serves 6-8

A special occasion vegetable

2 tablespoons butter
2 tablespoons flour
½ cup milk
3 egg yolks
2 (10 oz.) packages
  frozen spinach, thawed
  and squeezed dry
1 tablespoon chopped
  onion
¾ teaspoon salt
⅛ teaspoon pepper
3 egg whites

Preheat oven to 350°. Make thick white sauce of butter, flour, and milk. Remove saucepan from heat; whisk in egg yolks, one at a time. Stir in spinach, onion, salt, and pepper. Beat egg whites until stiff and gently fold into spinach mixture. Pour into greased and floured 1½-quart ring mold. Set ring into hot water bath. Bake 30 minutes or until firm to the touch. Loosen soufflé by running knife around edges of mold. Invert; fill center with mushrooms and onions. Serve at once.

Mushrooms and Onions in Sour Cream:

2 onions, thinly sliced
4 tablespoons butter,
  melted
1 pound small fresh
  mushrooms
1 cup sour cream
1 teaspoon lemon juice
1 teaspoon salt
Pepper
2 teaspoons chopped
  parsley

In a large saucepan, sauté onion in butter 6-8 minutes or until soft and translucent. Stir in mushrooms, cover pan; cook over moderate heat approximately 7 minutes. Add sour cream, lemon juice, salt, and pepper; stir until heated through; do not allow to boil. Season to taste and sprinkle with parsley.

RICH SQUASH CASSEROLE

Serves 10

20 yellow squash, sliced
1 onion, chopped
½ teaspoon salt
½ cup butter
2-3 teaspoons brown
  sugar
2 (8 oz.) cans sliced
  water chestnuts,
  drained
1 cup cracker crumbs
Butter

Preheat oven to 350°. Boil squash and onion in salted water 25 minutes or until tender; drain. Add butter and mash. Add brown sugar to taste. Layer squash mixture, water chestnuts, and cracker crumbs in deep ovenproof dish. Dot with butter. Bake 40-50 minutes or until brown.

Mrs. Michael L. McCullough
(JoAnne)

SPINACH MORNAY IN TOMATOES

Serves 8

3 (10 oz.) packages
  frozen chopped
  spinach, cooked and
  drained
Salt
Pepper
4 tablespoons butter,
  melted
3 tablespoons flour
⅛ teaspoon red pepper
1½ teaspoons Dijon
  mustard
4 tablespoons half and
  half
1 cup milk
3 tablespoons grated
  Swiss cheese
¼ cup grated Parmesan
  cheese
4 tablespoons half and
  half
4 tomatoes, halved
½ cup Parmesan cheese

Preheat oven to 350°. Season spinach with salt and pepper. In a saucepan combine butter, flour, red pepper, mustard, half and half, and milk; simmer 2 minutes. Add cheeses and half and half. Simmer 5 minutes; add spinach. Scoop out tomato halves and fill with spinach mixture. Sprinkle generously with Parmesan. Bake 15-20 minutes.

TOMATOES AND OKRA
Serves 12

2 pounds okra, cut in
  ½-inch slices
3 slices bacon, fried
  (reserve drippings)
1 Bell pepper (green),
  finely chopped
1 small onion, chopped
2 cloves garlic, minced
2 pounds fresh tomatoes,
  peeled and cubed
1 teaspoon salt
¼ teaspoon pepper

Sauté okra in bacon drippings; add Bell pepper, onion, and garlic; sauté lightly. Add bacon, tomatoes, salt, and pepper. Cover and simmer 15 minutes.

Mrs. John P. Mathis (Janet)

PARSNIP SOUFFLÉ
(Parsley, thyme)

2 pounds parsnips
1 large onion
2 tablespoons whipping
  cream
4 egg yolks
2 teaspoons chopped
  fresh parsley
2 teaspoons chopped
  fresh thyme
Salt
Pepper
4 egg whites, stiffly
  beaten

Preheat oven to 350°. Boil parsnips and onions until tender. Mash parsnips and chop onion finely. Beat egg yolks into parsnip and onion mixture. Add herbs and cream; season to taste with salt and pepper. Mix in beaten egg whites and put in large greased soufflé dish. Bake 30 minutes until golden and well risen. Serve immediately.

Elizabeth Peplow

STIR-FRIED VEGETABLES   Serves 6

2 tablespoons oil
1 cup julienned carrots
1 pint Brussels sprouts,
  sliced
1 cup julienned celery
2 zucchini, sliced
1 teaspoon cornstarch
4 teaspoons water
½ teaspoon salt
¼ teaspoon sugar
½ pound snow peas
1 teaspoon soy sauce

Pour oil in wok or saucepan; heat on high approximately 30 seconds; reduce heat to medium. Add carrots and Brussels sprouts; stir; cook 5 minutes. Add celery and zucchini; stir and cook 1 minute. Cover and continue cooking 3 minutes. Dissolve cornstarch in water; add to vegetables with salt and sugar, stirring to mix. Stir in snow peas; cover and cook 30 seconds. Add soy sauce and serve at once.

Miss Helen Corbitt

VEGETABLE MEDLEY   Serves 8-10

Oven-steamed ratatouille

2 Bell peppers (green),
  seeded and diced
1 eggplant, peeled and
  cubed
2 onions, coarsely
  chopped
2 tomatoes, coarsely
  chopped
1 pound fresh
  mushrooms, sliced
1 tablespoon fresh
  oregano
1½ teaspoons fresh
  thyme
Salt
Pepper
½ cup butter, melted
1 tablespoon water

Preheat oven to 350°. Combine all ingredients in 2-quart ovenproof dish. Cover and bake 45 minutes or until vegetables are tender.

Mrs. William C. McAfee (Louise)

TRI-COLOR VEGETABLE PÂTÉ
Serves 12

1 (10 oz.) package frozen
   spinach, thawed and
   squeezed dry
1 onion, finely chopped
3 tablespoons fresh dill or
   1½ teaspoons dried
   dillweed
2 tablespoons butter,
   melted
5 large eggs
1½ cups whipping cream
½ cup grated Parmesan
   cheese
1 teaspoon salt
⅛ teaspoon pepper
½ teaspoon nutmeg
1 pound carrots, peeled
   and cooked
1 (14 oz.) can artichoke
   hearts, drained

Preheat oven to 375°. Prepare loaf pan
by greasing, lining with a triple
thickness of wax paper, and greasing
again. Sauté spinach, onion, and ⅓ of
dill in butter until onion is translucent.
Combine eggs, cream, Parmesan, and
seasonings. Process spinach and 1 cup of
cream mixture until smoothly puréed.
Purée carrots with ⅓ of dill, and 1 cup
cream mixture. Purée remaining ⅓ of
dill and cream mixture with artichokes.
As each vegetable purée is completed,
gently spoon it in loaf pan. Bake pâté
set in hot water bath 1 hour 15
minutes or until a knife inserted in
center comes out clean. Serve cold. Pâté
can be unmolded when thoroughly
chilled.

Mrs. Harry J. McBrierty (Vikki)

VEGETABLE SPOON BREAD
Yields 1 (9-inch) pan

1 (10 oz.) package frozen
   chopped spinach,
   thawed and drained
   well
2 eggs, lightly beaten
1 (8¾ oz.) can cream-
   style corn
1 cup sour cream
½ cup butter, melted
¼ teaspoon salt
1 (8½ oz.) package corn
   muffin mix
1 cup grated Cheddar
   cheese

Preheat oven to 350°. In large bowl,
combine spinach, eggs, corn, sour
cream, butter, and salt; mix well. Add
corn muffin mix and ½ of cheese; stir
until thoroughly combined. Pour
mixture into greased ovenproof dish and
bake 30-35 minutes, until a toothpick
inserted in center comes out clean.
Sprinkle top with remaining cheese and
return to oven until cheese is melted.
Serve warm.

SPINACH-FILLED TURNIPS   Serves 4

4 turnips, peeled and
    steamed tender-crisp
1 (10 oz.) package frozen
    chopped spinach,
    cooked and drained
2 tablespoons butter,
    melted
6 tablespoons whipping
    cream
Salt
Pepper
1 tablespoon butter,
    melted

Preheat oven to 350⁰. Cut out centers of cooled turnips. Combine spinach and butter; stir fry over high heat 30 seconds. Add cream; cook until cream is reduced and slightly thickened. Season with salt and pepper. Fill turnips with spinach mixture. Pour butter over turnips and bake 15-20 minutes

Miss Helen Corbitt

SESAME ZUCCHINI   Serves 6

Toasty flavor and great color

4-6 zucchini, sliced
    diagonally
¼ cup finely chopped
    onion
1 clove garlic, minced
4 tablespoons butter,
    melted
½ cup halved cherry
    tomatoes or 1 small
    tomato, thinly sliced
1 teaspoon salt
Pepper
2 tablespoons sesame
    seeds, toasted
¼ cup finely chopped
    parsley

Blanch zucchini in boiling water 1 minute; drain. Sauté onion and garlic in butter. Add zucchini; cover and simmer 2 minutes. Add tomatoes; cover and simmer 1 minute. Season with salt and pepper. Sprinkle with sesame seeds and parsley. Toss and serve.

Miss Helen Corbitt

ZUCCHINI PROVENÇAL

Serves 8

4 zucchini, sliced
¼ teaspoon salt
2 tablespoons butter
½ Bell pepper (green),
  finely chopped
1 large tomato, chopped
½ onion, finely chopped
1-1½ cups grated sharp
  Cheddar cheese
1 cup breadcrumbs
Butter

Preheat oven to 350⁰. Parboil sliced zucchini with salt and water over low heat; drain. Place in ovenproof dish. In saucepan sauté Bell pepper, tomato, and onion until soft. Pour over zucchini. Sprinkle with cheese and breadcrumbs. Dot with butter. Bake 20 minutes.

Mrs. David Baxter Looney (Judy)

On November 6, 1979, the citizens of Dallas voted $2.25 million for the acquisition of land for a new concert hall for the Symphony. On August 3, 1982, voters approved a bond issue for over $28 million, or 60 percent of the cost of the Symphony's new home in the Arts District in downtown Dallas.

ZUCCHINI WITH PARMESAN

Serves 6-8

2 pounds zucchini, finely
  grated
1 tablespoon salt
2 shallots, chopped
3 tablespoons butter,
  melted
1 tablespoon oil
2 ounces Parmesan
  cheese, grated
Pepper

Place zucchini in colander; sprinkle with salt and drain 15 minutes. Rinse and press out excess water. Sauté shallots in butter and oil 1 minute. Add zucchini and toss over high heat 4-5 minutes or until tender. Toss with Parmesan until mixed. Sprinkle with pepper and serve immediately.

CREATIVE TOUCHES FOR FRESH VEGETABLES

Try a splash of color and a dash of spice to ease your way into exciting side dishes. Let these suggestions guide your creativity with vegetables.

- Cook tender-crisp.
- Toss with salad dressings and serve hot or cold.
- Add 2 teaspoons fresh herbs per 1 cup cooked vegetables.
- Combine any of the following: nuts, bacon bits, ham, celery seed, olives, capers, grated cheese, avocado, jicama, fresh tomato, mustard, horseradish, curry powder, spirits, thawed frozen peas, chives, cress, angastura bitters, celery root, red onion, sesame seeds, sprouts, turnips.

Try one of these suggestions with your favorite **cooked** vegetable.

ASPARAGUS:
- capers or green peppercorns
- fresh chervil, dill, and savory
- fresh nutmeg with or without cream sauce

BROCCOLI
- sesame oil and toasted sesame seed
- crumbled Feta cheese and steamed cherry tomatoes
- julienne strips of sautéed celery root and red Bell pepper with a lemony butter
- creamy vinaigrette served hot or cold

CARROTS
- slivered and sautéed with butter and rosemary
- steamed with sautéed onions, salt, dash of sugar; toss with fresh mint
- dressed with crème frâiche and tarragon

GREEN BEANS
- sautéed in olive oil with chopped garlic, black olives, droplets of lemon juice, and cracked pepper
- sautéed in walnut oil with toasted walnuts
- chopped fresh dill
- sautéed in olive oil with onion, garlic, tomato, and savory

SAUTÉED MUSHROOMS
- baked, covered for 10 minutes, sprinkled with parsley, dry sherry, bits of butter, salt, and pepper
- lemon juice, salt, pepper, fresh Parmesan, chopped parsley

ZUCCHINI
- shredded and sautéed in oil; splashed with vermouth, toasted pinenuts, salt, and pepper
- sauteed with garlic in butter; tossed with salt, pepper, parsley, and Parmesan cheese

Breads

CARAMEL CRUSTED CRANBERRY BREAD

Serves 16

2 cups flour
1 cup sugar
1½ teaspoons baking powder
1 teaspoon salt
½ teaspoon baking soda
4 tablespoons butter
1 egg, beaten
1 orange rind, grated
¾ cup orange juice
1½ cups golden raisins
1½ cups cranberries

Preheat oven to 350°. Sift flour, sugar, baking powder, salt, and baking soda together. Cut in butter until crumbly. Add egg, orange peel, and orange juice; stir only until evenly moist. Fold in raisins and cranberries. Bake in a greased 8-inch square pan 50-60 minutes or until done.

Mrs. W. Dwight Calkins (Linda)

Something magical happens during baking and produces a crunchy, chewy caramelized crust that is addictive.

CHEESE DATE BREAD

Yields 1 loaf

An ideal soup and salad accompaniment

1 cup boiling water
2 cups diced dates
⅓ cup butter
½ cup packed brown sugar
1 egg
1 cup grated Cheddar cheese
1½ cups sifted flour
½ teaspoon salt
1 teaspoon baking soda
½ cup whole wheat flour
½ cup chopped walnuts

Preheat oven to 350°. Pour boiling water over dates and set aside. Grease 9x5x3-inch loaf pan. In a mixing bowl, combine butter, brown sugar, and egg, beating until smooth. Stir in cheese and date mixture. Sift flour, salt, and soda. Beat flour mixture into bread batter. Add whole wheat flour and mix until smooth. Fold in walnuts. Pour into loaf pan. Bake 55 minutes. Turn out on wire rack. Do not attempt to slice bread until thoroughly cooled.

Mrs. Leslie D. Scott (Onita)

LEMON AND LIME BREAD
WITH CASHEWS
Yields 1 loaf

1 cup sugar
½ cup butter
2 eggs, lightly beaten
1¼ cups sifted flour
1 teaspoon baking
  powder
½ cup milk
¾ cup salted, toasted
  chopped cashews
Zest of 1 lemon, grated
Zest of 1 lime, grated
3 tablespoons fresh lemon
  juice
3 tablespoons fresh lime
  juice
7 tablespoons sugar

Preheat oven to 350°. Cream sugar and butter; add eggs. Combine flour, baking powder, and salt; sift together. Alternately add dry ingredients and milk to the creamed mixture, stirring well after each addition. Stir in nuts, lemon, and lime zest. Pour into a greased and floured loaf pan and bake 1 hour. Remove bread from pan. Make small holes in bread with toothpick. Mix lemon and lime juice with sugar; pour over bread while hot.

Mrs. R. C. Wynn (Melinda)

For an elegant luncheon or post-symphony supper to remember, serve this bread, Salmon Mousse with Vermouth Dressing, a chilled avocado soup, Romaine, Orange, and Watercress Salad, and Cold Lime Soufflé Maurice.

PERSIMMON BREAD
Yields 2 loaves
Full of brandy and unforgettable

3½ cups flour
1½ teaspoons salt
2 teaspoons baking soda
1 teaspoon mace
2-2½ cups sugar
1 cup butter, melted
4 eggs, beaten
⅔ cup brandy
2 cups persimmon purée
2 cups chopped nuts
2 cups raisins

Preheat oven to 350°. Sift dry ingredients together. Combine butter, eggs, brandy, persimmons, nuts, and raisins. Mix until smooth; fold in dry ingredients. Pour into greased and floured pans. Bake 1 hour.

HEAVENLY BRAN MUFFINS

Yields 36

1½ cups packed brown sugar
½ cup butter, melted
6 tablespoons molasses
6 eggs, lightly beaten
1 quart buttermilk
2 cups flour, sifted
¾ cup whole wheat flour
¼ cup quick-cooking oatmeal
1 tablespoon baking soda
1½ teaspoons baking powder
4 cups any coarse bran cereal
1 cup natural bran
1 cup chopped raisins or chopped dates (optional)

Preheat oven to 400°. Add brown sugar, butter, and molasses to eggs; mix well. Stir in remaining ingredients just to blend. Fill greased muffin tins ⅔ full. Bake 15 minutes or until done.

Mrs. James Hill (Sandy)

Batter may be kept up to 3 weeks in the refrigerator.

FRESH APPLE COFFEE CAKE

Serves 6

1 cup flour
2 teaspoons baking powder
½ teaspoon salt
1 tablespoon butter
1 cup sugar
1 egg, beaten lightly
2 cups diced apples

Topping:
½ cup sugar
2 teaspoons cinnamon
Butter

Preheat oven to 375°. Combine flour, baking powder, and salt; set aside. Cream butter and sugar; add egg. Fold flour mixture into egg mixture. Add diced apples. Spread into 8-inch square ovenproof dish that has been greased and floured. Sprinkle with topping. Dot with butter. Bake 30 minutes.

Mrs. Walter N. Skinner (Judy)

CREAM CHEESE BRAIDS

Yields 4 loaves

Dough:
1 cup sour cream
½ cup sugar
1 teaspoon salt
½ cup butter, melted
2 packages yeast
½ cup warm water
2 eggs, beaten
4 cups flour

Heat sour cream over low heat; stir in sugar, salt, and butter; cool to lukewarm. Sprinkle yeast over water in large dish stirring until yeast dissolves. Add sour cream mixture, eggs, and flour; mix well. Cover tightly; refrigerate overnight.

The next day, divide dough into 4 equal parts; roll out each part on a well floured board into a 12 x 8-inch rectangle. Spread ¼ of cream cheese filling on each rectangle; roll up jelly-roll fashion, beginning at long sides. Pinch edges together and fold ends under slightly; place rolls seam side down on greased baking sheets.

Alternately cut dough diagonally at 2-inch intervals about ⅔ of the way through to resemble a braid. Cover and let rise until doubled in bulk, approximately 1 hour. Bake at 350° 12-15 minutes. Spread with glaze while warm.

Cream Cheese Filling:
2 (8 oz.) packages cream cheese, room temperature
¾ cup sugar
1 egg, beaten
1 teaspoon vanilla extract
1 teaspoon almond extract

Combine cream cheese and sugar in small dish. Add egg and extracts; mix well.

(Continued on next page)

148

Glaze:
2 cups powdered sugar
¼ cup milk
1 teaspoon vanilla extract
1 teaspoon almond
extract

Combine all ingredients; mix well.
Mrs. James C. Hill (Sandy)

NORWEGIAN KRINGLE   Yields 2
Ideal for Christmas gifts

Pastry Base:
½ cup butter
1 cup flour
1 tablespoon water

Preheat oven to 350⁰. Cut butter into
flour; sprinkle with 1 tablespoon water
and mix well. Pat into two 3x12-inch
strips on an ungreased baking sheet; set
aside.

Chou Topping:
½ cup butter
1 cup water
1 cup flour
3 eggs
1 teaspoon almond
extract

Bring butter and water to a boil;
remove from heat; whisk in flour all at
once. Cook and stir several minutes
over very low heat. Remove from heat
and beat in eggs one at a time; add
almond extract. Spread the chou paste
over the pastry strips and bake 50-60
minutes.

Icing:
1 cup powdered sugar
½ teaspoon almond
extract
1-2 tablespoons milk

Mix icing ingredients. Drizzle over
cooled Kringle. Sprinkle with optional
almonds and dot with cherries.
Mrs. Kipp Murray (Gwen)

Optional Garnishes:
¼ cup slivered almonds
¼ cup maraschino
cherries, halved

*Cut into 2-inch sections and serve for
brunch or cut into 1-inch strips and
use as a dessert cookie.*

GOLDEN RAISIN SCONES   Yields 12

2 cups flour
2½ teaspoons baking
powder
½ teaspoon salt
2 tablespoons sugar
½ cup butter
½ cup golden raisins
5 tablespoons milk
2 eggs, reserve 1
tablespoon egg white
for glaze
2 tablespoons sugar

Preheat oven to 450⁰. Sift flour, baking powder, salt, and sugar; cut in butter; stir in raisins and milk. Lightly beat eggs and stir into dough. Dough will be sticky. Roll out on a floured board; cut into 3-inch squares and then crosswise into triangles. Space on a greased baking sheet; brush tops with reserved egg white and sprinkle with sugar. Bake 10-15 minutes. Serve warm with butter.

Mrs. Jim Grubbs (Mary)

Although a natural choice for brunch or tea early in the day, scones work equally well at dinnertime with Baked Ham with Cumberland Sauce, or any main dish hinting of a sweet-spicy flavor.

GRANDMA'S BISCUITS   Yields 12

"Grandma" worked at the famous San Jacinto Inn, turning out hundreds of these feather-light biscuits daily.

2 cups flour
1 tablespoon baking
powder
½ teaspoon salt
4 teaspoons sugar
¾ cup shortening
¾ cup milk

Preheat oven to 450⁰. Combine flour, baking powder, salt, and sugar. Cut in shortening; add milk and stir lightly. Dough will be very soft. Drop by heaping tablespoons onto an ungreased baking sheet. Bake 10 minutes or until tops brown lightly.

Large ones make great shortcakes!

BAGELS

1 package yeast
1 tablespoon sugar
2-2½ cups lukewarm
   water
8 cups sifted flour
1½ teaspoons salt
¼ cup sugar
¼ cup oil
2 eggs, beaten

Dissolve yeast and 1 tablespoon sugar in ½ cup water. Sift flour and salt; add yeast mixture, sugar, salad oil, eggs, and enough water to make a soft dough. Knead until smooth and elastic. Let rise in warm place until doubled in size. Punch down and divide into 24 parts. Bring water to boil in very large saucepan. Roll each piece of dough into a rope ¾ inch in diameter. Flour hands and counter if necessary. Join ends to form a ring. Drop into boiling water without crowding. Cook until they float to the surface, about 3 minutes. Remove with slotted spoon and place on well-greased baking sheet. Bake at 375° 20-25 minutes or until nicely browned.

Mr. W. Dwight Calkins

PARTY-PERFECT
REFRIGERATOR ROLLS

½ cup boiling water
½ cup shortening
⅓ cup sugar
1 teaspoon salt
1 egg, beaten
1 package yeast
¼ cup cold water
3 cups flour

Pour boiling water over shortening, sugar, and salt. Blend and cool until mixture is lukewarm. Stir in egg. Let yeast stand in cold water 5 minutes. Combine ½ flour with shortening mixture; add yeast mixture. Blend in remaining flour until smooth. Let rise until doubled; punch down. Cover and refrigerate at least 8 hours. Remove from refrigerator 3 hours before cooking. Knead dough; place in greased muffin tins. Let rise in warm place. Bake at 400° 10-15 minutes.

Mrs. Robert A. Smith, Jr. (Juanita)

LAHVASH -
ARMENIAN CRACKER BREAD

Yields 12 rounds

1 cup warm water
1 package yeast
½ teaspoon sugar
4 tablespoons butter,
    melted
1½ teaspoons salt
½ teaspoon sugar
3¼-3¾ cups flour
Butter

Combine water, yeast, and sugar; let stand 5 minutes. Add butter, salt, sugar, and 2 cups flour. Beat until smooth, adding additional flour gradually to make a stiff dough. Knead dough by hand or with dough hook 10 minutes or until dough is elastic. Coat dough with butter and place in a buttered bowl. Put in a warm place; let rise until doubled in bulk, approximately 2 hours. Divide dough into 12 pieces; form into balls. At this point the dough may be frozen. Roll the balls into 10½-inch rounds. Place on baking sheet and bake at 350° 15-20 minutes. Allow lahvash to cool on wire racks.

Mrs. A. Earl Cullum, Jr. (Bobbie)

The December, 1976 announcement of Eduardo Mata's appointment as Music Director of the Dallas Symphony was made in Mexico City, where Mata was conducting the New Philharmonic Orchestra of London. Only 34 years old, Mata was already in his twelfth year as an orchestral director. At 22, he had become Music Director of the Guadalajara Symphony Orchestra in his native Mexico. At 24, he had taken control of the Orquesta Filharmonica at the National University of Mexico. Mata brought extensive experience, vigor, and his own brand of leadership to bear on the task of guiding the musical future of the DSO.

IRISH MONKEY BREAD

Yields 1 loaf

Long a caterer's secret

6 cups flour
½ cup sugar
2 teaspoons salt
1 cup mashed potatoes
½ cup butter
2 eggs
1 cup milk, scalded
2 packages yeast
½ cup butter, melted

Sift together flour, sugar, and salt. Mix hot potatoes and butter in mixer; add eggs. Let milk cook to lukewarm, 105-110°; dissolve yeast in milk. Add milk and yeast to potato mixture. Add flour mixture as long as mixer will mix, then work in remaining flour by hand. Work dough until smooth and elastic. Place in a greased bowl and turn to coat. Cover and let rise until doubled in volume. Roll dough into 1-inch balls. Dip each piece in melted butter and place in ring mold pan at least 4 inches deep. Let rise until double; bake at 350° for 10 minutes, then bake at 400° until done, approximately 30-40 minutes.

Mrs. Joe Mullins, Jr. (Bette)

To freeze bake 10 minutes at 350°, then 10-15 minutes at 400°. Immediately wrap in foil and freeze.

Since September of 1977, Eduardo Mata has been the Symphony's Music Director. Under Maestro Mata, the DSO signed a new recording contract with RCA Victor. And the DSO under Maestro Mata received a "Grammy" nomination for "The Works of Richard Strauss."

CRACKED
WHEAT CARROT BREAD

Yields 2 loaves

Hearty texture with a hint of sweet

2 carrots, shredded
5½ cups flour
4 tablespoons butter,
  softened
¼ cup packed light
  brown sugar
2 teaspoons salt
1 package yeast
⅓ cup warm water
  (105-115⁰)
⅔ cup ice water
⅔ cup cold milk
¾ cup fine cracked
  wheat

Blend carrots, flour, butter, sugar, and salt thoroughly. Dissolve yeast in warm water; pour into carrot mixture. Combine ice water and milk; slowly pour into carrot mixture while stirring constantly. Mix until a rough, coherent mass forms. Add cracked wheat slowly. Mix until dough forms a ball, then knead. Shape into small ball; place in a greased bowl or lightly floured, 1-gallon plastic bag. Let rise 1-1½ hours or until dough has doubled. Shape into 2 loaves. Place each loaf in a greased, 6-cup loaf pan; let rest 45 minutes or until dough rises above pans. Bake at 375⁰ 35-45 minutes. Remove from pans and cool on wire racks.

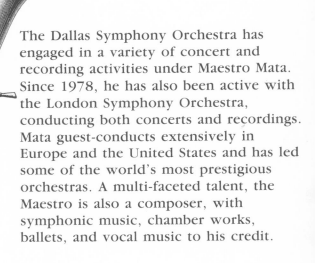

The Dallas Symphony Orchestra has engaged in a variety of concert and recording activities under Maestro Mata. Since 1978, he has also been active with the London Symphony Orchestra, conducting both concerts and recordings. Mata guest-conducts extensively in Europe and the United States and has led some of the world's most prestigious orchestras. A multi-faceted talent, the Maestro is also a composer, with symphonic music, chamber works, ballets, and vocal music to his credit.

HERBED CHEESE AND ONION BREAD

Yields 1 loaf

1½ cups whole wheat flour
1 teaspoon salt
1 cup grated sharp Cheddar cheese
½ cup finely chopped onion
1 teaspoon crushed rosemary
½ teaspoon dill
¼ teaspoon marjoram
¼ teaspoon thyme
1 package yeast
½ cup chicken broth
½ cup lukewarm milk
1 egg, lightly beaten
2 tablespoons honey
1½ cups all purpose flour
1 egg yolk
2 tablespoons water

Sift together whole wheat flour and salt. Add cheese, onion, rosemary, dill, marjoram, and thyme; mix well. In a small dish sprinkle yeast over ¼ cup broth, set aside; let stand 10 minutes. Combine milk, yeast mixture, remaining ¼ cup broth, egg, and honey. Add to whole wheat flour mixture, stirring until well blended. Gradually beat in as much remaining flour as possible, kneading 8-10 minutes or until smooth and elastic. Form into a ball; place in buttered dish and turn to coat. Cover with towel; place in large dish with warm water. Allow to rise 30 minutes. Punch down; knead 1 minute. Place in a buttered loaf pan and chill uncovered at least 8 hours. When ready to bake, allow dough to stand in a warm place 30 minutes; preheat oven to 350°. Combine egg yolk and water; brush over top of dough. Bake 50 minutes.

Mrs. Allen E. Cullum (Sissy)

This has enough zing to add excitement to simple soups or roasted meats.

HERB ORANGE BREAD

Yields 1 loaf

(Parsley, chives, French tarragon)

1 package active dry
  yeast
¼ cup lukewarm water
⅓ cup frozen orange
  juice concentrate,
  thawed, undiluted
¼ cup hot water
¼ cup sugar
3 tablespoons melted
  shortening
2 teaspoons salt
3 cups flour, divided
1 egg
½ teaspoon grated
  orange rind
⅓ cup minced fresh
  parsley
⅓ cup minced fresh
  chives
3 tablespoons fresh
  French tarragon

Sprinkle yeast over lukewarm water, stir until dissolved. Into large bowl pour undiluted orange concentrate, hot water, sugar, shortening, and salt; stir well. When mixture is warm, but not hot, stir in 1 cup flour, then yeast. Add egg and orange rind; beat hard. Stir in 1½ cups flour. Sprinkle rolling surface with remaining flour. Knead dough, adding flour as needed, until dough is soft and satiny. Shape into ball. Place in lightly oiled bowl; cover. Let rise until double in bulk, about 2 hours. Punch down and let rest 5 minutes. Pat out dough on board. Sprinkle with herbs. Roll up like jelly roll. Place in lightly greased 9 x 5 x 3-inch loaf pan; cover. Let rise about 1 hour. Bake at 350° for 40-45 minutes.

Ethel W. Watchorn

I.M. Pei, the designer of Dallas concert hall, is one of the world's most illustrious architects. Pei designed, with his partners, the City Hall, One Dallas Center, and the ARCO Tower in Dallas. His best known works include the John Fitzgerald Kennedy Library in Cambridge, Massachusetts and the East Wing of the National Gallery in Washington, D.C.

JALAPEÑO CORN BREAD   Serves 20
Truly Texan

1½ cups yellow cornmeal
3 teaspoons baking
  powder
½ teaspoon salt
1 cup grated Cheddar
  cheese
1 cup grated onion
5 large jalapeños, finely
  chopped
3 eggs, lightly beaten
½ cup oil
1 cup sour cream
1½ cups corn or 1 (8
  oz.) can cream-style
  corn

Preheat oven to 400°. Combine cornmeal, baking powder, and salt. Stir in cheese, onions, and jalapeños. Add eggs, oil, sour cream, and corn; mix well. Pour into greased 9x13-inch ovenproof dish; bake 20-30 minutes or until straw comes out clean.

CORNMEAL CHEESE BREAD   Yields 2 loaves

1 package yeast
¼ cup lukewarm water
8 ounces sharp Cheddar
  cheese, grated
5 cups flour
5 tablespoons butter,
  softened
2 tablespoons sugar
1 tablespoon salt
2 eggs
6-8 drops hot pepper
  sauce
1¼ cups ice water
1 cup yellow cornmeal

Dissolve yeast in water. Knead together cheese, flour, butter, sugar, and salt. Add yeast mixture, eggs, and hot pepper sauce, mixing thoroughly. Continue mixing; pour ice water in as fast as flour mixture absorbs it. Add cornmeal and continue mixing until dough begins to form a ball. With floured hands, remove dough and shape into ball. Place in a greased bowl or lightly floured, 1-gallon plastic bag. Let rise in warm place 1-1½ hours until dough has doubled. Remove from bag and shape into 2 loaves. Place each loaf in greased, 6-cup loaf pan; let rise 1 hour or until dough rises above top of pans. Bake at 375° 35-40 minutes. Remove from pans and cool on wire racks.

BASIL-PINEAPPLE JELLY
(Basil)

Yields 3 (8 oz.) jars

¾ cup water
¼ cup chopped fresh
basil leaves, packed
1 cup unsweetened
pineapple juice,
strained
3 cups sugar
1 drop yellow food
coloring
1 drop red food coloring
3 ounces liquid pectin

Bring water and basil leaves to a boil and immediately remove from heat; cover and set aside for 10 minutes. Strain before using. Combine pineapple juice, lemon juice, and sugar in 3-quart pan; bring to a boil and cook until sugar is dissolved, stirring constantly. Remove from heat; skim foam and stir in food colorings. Quickly add pectin, stirring constantly. Return to heat and boil for 1 minute. Remove from heat; skim and pour into hot, sterile jars and seal.

Mrs. William L. Furneaux

HERB BUTTERS

½ cup butter, softened
1½ tablespoons minced
fresh herbs*
1 teaspoon fresh lemon
juice

Mix all ingredients and store in glazed, butter pots.

*Simple herb butters may use French tarragon, sweet marjoram, garlic, garlic chives, onion chives, rosemary, sage, basil, borage, winter savory, chervil, dill, and thyme.

Combination herb butters may use 2 teaspoons each of parsley, chives, and nasturtium leaves or cress; 2 tablespoons chervil and 2 garlic cloves, crushed; 1 teaspoon thyme, 1½ teaspoons savory, and 1 garlic clove, crushed; 2 teaspoons parsley, ½ teaspoon basil, ½ teaspoon chives, and 1 tablespoon lemon rind; 2 teaspoons marjoram, 2½ teaspoons caraway seeds, and 1 teaspoon parsley.

Mrs. William L. Furneaux

Desserts

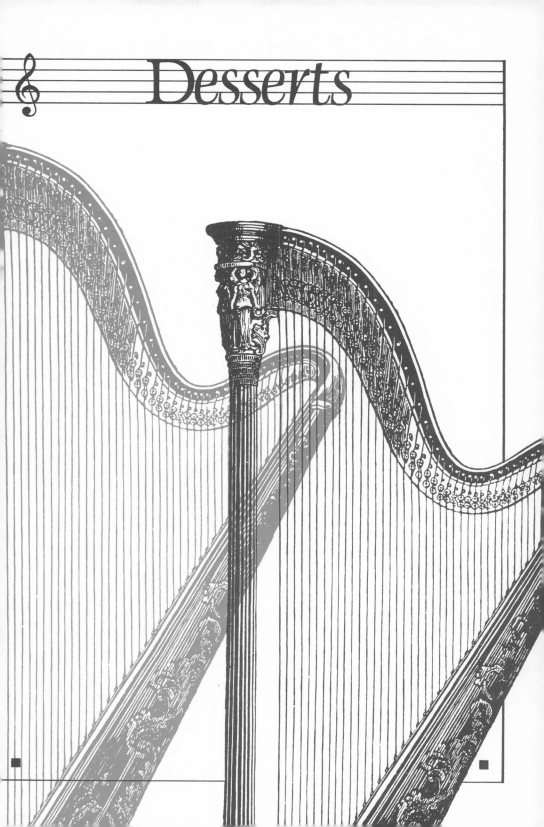

FRESH ORANGE CAKE   Serves 10-12

1 cup sugar
1 cup butter
2 eggs
2½ cups flour
1 teaspoon baking
    powder
1 teaspoon baking soda
⅛ teaspoon salt
1 cup sour cream
1 teaspoon vanilla extract
1 cup chopped pecans
2 orange rinds, grated

Preheat oven to 350°. Cream sugar and butter, add eggs. Combine dry ingredients and add alternately with sour cream. Add vanilla, nuts, and rind. Bake in greased, floured tube pan 1 hour, or until toothpick comes out clean.

Syrup:
Juice of 2 oranges
1 cup sugar

Combine ingredients and boil 5 minutes. Pour syrup over hot cake; let cool in pan.

Mrs. Ralph Ross (Lee)

For an impressive touch, slice Fresh Orange Cake horizontally into 3 layers. Fill and top with 2 cups whipping cream, whipped with ¼ cup confectioner's sugar and 3 tablespoons orange liqueur. Add 1 pint sliced fresh strawberries between the layers, saving some gorgeous ones for the top.

BLACK FOREST CAKE   Serves 12

2 egg whites
½ cup sugar
1¾ cups cake flour
1 cup sugar
¾ teaspoon baking soda
1 teaspoon salt
⅓ cup oil
½ cup milk
2 egg yolks
2 ounces unsweetened
   chocolate, melted
½ cup milk

Preheat oven to 350⁰. Beat egg whites until soft peaks form. Gradually add ½ cup sugar, beating until stiff. Sift together dry ingredients; add oil and ½ cup milk; beat 1 minute. Add egg yolks, chocolate, and remaining ½ cup milk; beat 1 minute. Gently fold in egg whites. Pour into 2 greased and floured 9-inch layer pans. Bake 30-35 minutes. Cool 10 minutes; remove from pans. Cool thoroughly and split layers in half.

Cherry Filling:
1 (20 oz.) can pitted tart
   cherries, drained
½ cup port wine
1 tablespoon kirsch
¼ teaspoon almond
   extract

Combine cherries, wine, kirsch, and almond extract. Chill several hours; drain before using.

Chocolate Mousse:
3 ounces semi-sweet
   chocolate
3 tablespoons kirsch
1 egg, beaten
1 cup whipping cream,
   whipped
2 tablespoons sugar

Melt chocolate and kirsch over low heat. Beat chocolate mixture into egg; fold in cream and sugar. Chill 2 hours.

Butter Frosting:
6 tablespoons butter
1 cup powdered sugar
2 tablespoons half and
   half
1½ teaspoons vanilla
   extract
1 cup powdered sugar

Cream butter and 1 cup powdered sugar. Beat in half and half and vanilla. Add remaining powdered sugar and enough half and half to make spreading consistency; chill.

(Continued on next page)

Filling and Frosting Cream:
2 cups whipping cream
2 tablespoons sugar
1 teaspoon vanilla extract

Garnish:
Powdered sugar
Whipping cream, whipped
Maraschino cherries
Chocolate curls

To assemble cake, spread ½ cup Butter Frosting on cut side of 1 cake layer. With remaining frosting form 1 collar ½ inch wide and ¾ inch high around outside edge of same layer. Make another collar 2 inches from outside edge. Chill 30 minutes. Fill inner space with cherry filling. Spread second layer with chocolate mousse and place on top of first layer. Chill 30 minutes. Whip cream, sugar, and vanilla. Spread third cake layer with 1½ cups cream. Place on top of second layer. Top with remaining cake layer. Frost sides with remaining ¼ cup cream. Sift powdered sugar on top. Garnish with cream, cherries, and curls; chill.

Mrs. Charles R. Gibbs (Harriett)

JACK HORNER CAKES
Yields 3 dozen

½ cup shortening
1 cup packed light brown sugar
2 egg yolks, beaten
1 cup flour
½ teaspoon mace
1½ teaspoons vanilla extract
2 egg whites, stiffly beaten
½ cup finely chopped nuts
36 maraschino cherries, pitted

Preheat oven to 350°. Cream shortening and brown sugar until very light. Add beaten yolks to creamed mixture. Sift together flour and mace; add to creamed mixture, combining well. Add vanilla, mixing well. Fold in egg whites. In well greased 1¾-inch muffin tin, sprinkle chopped nuts; cover with small amount of batter; place a cherry in center and cover with more batter. Sprinkle top with nuts. Bake 20 minutes.

Use 1-inch muffin liner to make smaller cakes.

ROSE GERANIUM CAKE
(Rose geranium)

1 cup butter
2 cups sugar
6 eggs, divided
2 cups flour, divided
15 rose geranium leaves

Cream together butter, sugar, and 2 eggs. Add 1 cup flour and 2 eggs; mix well. Scrape bottom and sides of bowl and add 1 cup flour and 2 eggs; beat briefly, scrape bowl and beat briskly a moment. Generously butter bottom and sides of tube pan and cover with rose geranium leaves. (Leaves should be washed, patted dry and tough stems removed. Front side of leaf should be against the butter.) Pour batter into tube pan and put into cold oven. Bake 1 hour at 350°. Test for doneness; if not done, test every 2 minutes. Cool 10 minutes on rack; place cake plate on top of tube pan and invert quickly.
Mrs. William L. Furneaux (Lane)

Serve with vanilla custard sauce.

STRAWBERRY ROSE POUND CAKE
(Rose geranium)

1 cup butter
3 cups sugar
½ cup shortening
6 eggs, beaten
½ teaspoon baking
  powder
3 cups flour
1 cup milk
1 tablespoon lemon peel,
  grated
1 tablespoon orange peel,
  grated
1 teaspoon vanilla
4-5 rose geranium leaves

Preheat oven to 325⁰. Cream butter, sugar, and shortening; add eggs. Sift together baking powder and flour; add to butter mixture alternately with milk. Stir in lemon and orange zest with vanilla. Line a greased, floured tube pan with rose geranium leaves. Pour in batter. Bake 1 hour and 35-45 minutes or until done. Cool 10 minutes; turn out onto cooling rack for another 10 minutes. While slightly warm, add glaze.

Glaze:
1 pint fresh strawberries,
  sliced and sweetened or
  1 (10 oz.) package
  frozen strawberries
½ cup fresh orange juice
3 tablespoons lemon juice
1½ cups sugar
3 tablespoons rum
Whipping cream,
  whipped

Mix together strawberries, orange juice, and lemon juice in saucepan; bring to boil. Stirring constantly, add in sugar; cool 10 minutes; add rum. Pierce cake with fork and pour glaze over cake. Top with whipped cream.

LANE CAKE

3¼ cups cake flour
2 teaspoons baking
  powder
1/16 teaspoon salt
1 cup butter, softened
2 cups sugar
2 teaspoons vanilla
  extract
8 egg whites
1 cup milk

Preheat oven to 375°. Sift together dry ingredients. Cream butter, sugar, and vanilla. Add egg whites, 2 at a time, beating after each addition. Fold in flour mixture alternately with milk; begin and end with dry ingredients. Pour into 4 ungreased 9-inch, round layer cake pans lined with wax paper. Bake 20 minutes or until edges shrink slightly from sides of pans and top springs back when gently pressed. Cool on wire racks about 5 minutes; turn out of pans; remove wax paper; turn right-side up; cool completely. Add Lane-Cake Filling between each layer; top with White Frosting. Cover; store in cool place. If refrigerated, bring to room temperature before serving.

Lane Cake Filling:
8 egg yolks
1 cup sugar
½ cup butter, softened
1 cup finely chopped
  seedless raisins
⅓ cup bourbon or
  brandy
1 teaspoon vanilla extract

In 2-quart saucepan, beat egg yolks; add sugar and butter. Cook, stirring constantly over moderate heat, until thick. Remove from heat; stir in raisins, bourbon or brandy, and vanilla. Cool slightly.

White Frosting:
½ cup sugar
¼ cup white corn syrup
⅛ teaspoon salt
2 tablespoons water
2 egg whites
½ teaspoon vanilla
  extract

In 1-quart saucepan, mix sugar, syrup, salt, and water. Stir over moderately low heat several times to dissolve sugar. Boil to thread stage (242° on candy thermometer). Beat egg whites to soft peaks. Gradually beat about half of syrup mixture into beaten whites. Place saucepan with remaining syrup in

(Continued on next page)

another saucepan of hot water off heat to keep warm. Continue beating egg white mixture until thick and fluffy. Gradually beat in remaining warm syrup and vanilla. Continue to beat, if necessary, until mixture holds stiff, shiny peaks.

Mrs. William L. Furneaux (Lane)

FROZEN KAHLÚA CAKE   Serves 12

A must!

¾ cup butter, softened
2 cups sugar
¾ cup cocoa
4 egg yolks
1 teaspoon baking soda
2 tablespoons cold water
½ cup cold coffee
½ cup Kahlúa
1⅓ cups flour
2 tablespoons vanilla
  extract
4 egg whites, beaten

Glaze:
1 cup powdered sugar
½ cup Kahlúa

Topping:
1 cup whipping cream,
  whipped

Preheat oven to 325°. Cream butter and sugar. Add cocoa and egg yolks. Dissolve soda in water and combine with coffee and Kahlúa; add to batter, alternating with flour. Add vanilla and fold in stiffly beaten egg whites. Grease and flour bundt pan. Pour in batter; remove air bubbles. Bake 1 hour. Combine glaze ingredients and pour over warm cake; cover with foil and freeze. About 1 hour before serving, remove from freezer and ice with whipped cream.

CHOCOLATE MOCHA CAKE   Serves 10-12

¾ cup shortening
4 eggs, beaten
2 cups sugar
2 cups sifted flour
1 cup cold coffee
3 ounces semi-sweet
    chocolate, melted
1 teaspoon baking soda
2 tablespoons water

Preheat oven to 375⁰. Cream shortening; add eggs and sugar; beat well. Add flour alternately with coffee; add chocolate. Dissolve baking soda in water; add to mixture. Pour into 2 greased and floured 8-inch layer pans. Bake 30-35 minutes or until straw inserted in center comes out clean.

Mocha Frosting:
2 cups powdered sugar
3 tablespoons cocoa
¾ cup butter
8 teaspoons hot coffee
3 tablespoons vanilla
    extract

Sift powdered sugar and cocoa together. Cream butter; add dry ingredients alternately with coffee and vanilla. Mix well. Ice on cooled cake.

For special guests spread Hazelnut Filling on each layer before icing with Mocha Frosting and sprinkle cake liberally with ¾ cup coarsely chopped toasted hazelnuts.

Hazelnut Filling:
1¼ cups skinned
    hazelnuts
5 tablespoons light corn
    syrup
3 tablespoons brandy
1¼ cup confectioner's
    sugar
6 tablespoons butter

Toast hazelnuts on baking sheet in 350⁰ oven for 10-15 minutes or until golden brown; cool. Grind or process nuts until they become pastry; add corn syrup and brandy. Beat with confectioner's sugar and butter until thoroughly mixed and creamy. Chill briefly to firm.

Hazelnuts may be purchased as filberts in well-stocked grocery stores. If only nuts with skins are available. rub skins off while nuts are hot from toasting.

CASSATA ALLA SICILIANA
Serves 10

1 (9-inch) pound cake
1 pound ricotta or large
  curd cottage cheese
1 tablespoon whipping
  cream
¼ cup sugar
3 tablespoons orange
  liqueur or agnostura
  bitters
3 tablespoons coarsely
  chopped preserved
  fruits
¼ cup coarsely chopped
  semi-sweet chocolate

Slice the pound cake horizontally into
¾-inch slices, leveling the top as
necessary. Process cheese, cream, sugar,
and liqueur until smooth. Fold in the
fruits and chocolate. Fill the layers of
pound cake with the cheese mixture,
leaving the top plain. Refrigerate several
hours or until firm. Frost with Mocha
Icing and refrigerate overnight to blend
flavors.

Mocha Icing:
12 ounces semi-sweet
  chocolate
¾ cup strong coffee
1 cup butter

Melt chocolate with coffee, stirring
constantly. Off heat, beat in the butter
bit by bit until smooth. Chill until
thick enough to spread.

NORWEGIAN APPLE PIE
Serves 16

1½ cups sugar
1 cup flour
2 teaspoons baking
  powder
½ teaspoon salt
2 eggs
2 tablespoons butter,
  melted
½ teaspoon vanilla
  extract
2 cups diced apples
1 cup chopped pecans
1 cup whipping cream,
  whipped (optional)

Preheat oven to 350°. Combine sugar,
flour, baking powder, and salt. Beat in
eggs 1 at a time. Add vanilla and
butter; mix until smooth. Fold in
apples and nuts. Spread into two 8-inch
greased and floured pie plates. Bake 35
minutes. Serve with dollops of whipped
cream.

Mrs. Robert E. Glaze (Ruth)

RUM BABAS
Serves 6-8

Babas:
1 package yeast
3 tablespoons lukewarm
  water
1¾ cups flour
3 eggs, beaten
1 teaspoon salt
1 tablespoon sugar
⅔ cup dried currants
¼ cup water
¼ cup rum

Sprinkle yeast over lukewarm water and let stand until dissolved. Sift flour into a large mixing bowl and make a well in center. Add yeast mixture, eggs, salt, and sugar; work together with hands. Beat dough with hands, raising dough with fingers and slapping it back into bowl, for 6 minutes or until smooth and elastic. Cover with damp cloth and let stand in warm place to rise 1 hour or until doubled in size. Soak dried currants in water and rum. Preheat oven to 400⁰. Butter 8 dariole molds; chill in freezer and butter again. Beat softened butter into risen dough and fill molds half full. Set on baking sheet in warm place; cover with cloth and let rise for 20 minutes, or until molds are almost full. Remove cloth and bake 20 minutes or until babas begin to pull away from sides of molds.

Syrup:
9 tablespoons butter,
  softened
1¼ cups sugar
2 cups water
⅓ cup rum

In saucepan heat sugar and water over low heat, stirring continuously, until sugar is dissolved; boil 2-3 minutes until syrup is clear. Remove from heat. Place babas in hot syrup, turning several times. Babas will swell and be very shiny. Remove with slotted spoon and place on rack. Sprinkle remaining syrup and rum over babas just before serving. Store in tightly covered container for 24 hours.

Anne Willan

DEVON TRIFLE
Serves 10

Jelly Rolls:
5 eggs, separated
½ teaspoon salt
⅓ cup sugar
1½ teaspoons orange rind
2 tablespoons orange
  juice
⅓ cup cornstarch
⅓ cup flour
1½ cups strawberry jam
  or raspberry jam

Preheat oven to 375⁰. Whip egg whites to a froth; add salt and continue beating to form peaks. Gradually add sugar, beating until meringue is stiff but not dry. In another dish, beat egg yolks, orange rind, and juice until light in color. Lightly fold in meringue, cornstarch, and flour. Turn into a greased and floured 10x15x1-inch jelly roll pan. Bake 12-15 minutes. Place cake on wax paper equal in length and spread with jam. Starting at wide end, roll cake into a jelly roll.

Soft Custard:
3 cups milk
8 large egg yolks, beaten
1 cup sugar
¼ teaspoon salt
½ cup flour
2 teaspoons vanilla
  extract
4 tablespoons butter

Yields 4 cups
Heat milk to boiling. In a saucepan combine eggs, sugar, and salt; blend in flour. Slowly stir in milk, cooking over medium heat until custard boils and thickens. Remove from heat; stir in vanilla and butter. Cool; cover top with plastic wrap. Refrigerate until ready to use.

1 Jelly Roll filled with
  strawberry or raspberry
  jam
⅓ cup orange juice or
  sweet wine
¾ cup sugar
3 ounces water
4 ounces chocolate chips
1 pint strawberries, sliced
¼ cup strawberry or
  raspberry jam
2 cups custard
1 cup whipping cream,
  whipped

Slice jelly roll and lay in shallow glass dish or trifle bowl. Moisten lightly with juice or wine. Combine sugar and water over low heat to dissolve sugar; add chocolate, stirring until melted. Spread jam and then chocolate mixture over jelly rolls. Chill; spoon sliced strawberries evenly; cover with custard and pipe with whipped cream flavored to taste. Decorate with chocolate leaves and/or fresh strawberries.

CHOCOLATE MARBLE CHEESECAKE   Serves 12

4 ounces unsweetened
chocolate
4 (8 oz.) packages cream
cheese, softened
1 teaspoon vanilla extract
¼ teaspoon almond
extract
1¾ cups sugar
4 eggs
⅓ cup graham cracker
crumbs

Preheat oven to 325°. Melt chocolate in double boiler and set aside. Blend cream cheese until smooth; beat in extracts and sugar. Add eggs, one at a time, while beating. Remove ⅓ of mixture and set aside. Add chocolate to remaining cream cheese mixture and beat until smooth. Butter an 8 x 3-inch spring form pan, including sides and rim. Alternate large spoonfuls of chocolate batter and small spoonfuls of white batter into pan with some of white batter on outside. Bake 1 hour 30 minutes or until top is golden brown. Turn off oven and leave cheesecake in oven 30 minutes. Place cheesecake on rack and let cool 2-3 hours. Do not cool in refrigerator. Invert cake; remove pan and sprinkle bottom with crumbs. Carefully invert once again so cake will be upright. Refrigerate 5-6 hours. Serve very cold.

Miss Helen Corbitt

Cheesecake freezes perfectly.

CHEESECAKE WITH
RASPBERRY SAUCE

Serves 8-10

Crust:
1½ cups graham cracker
  crumbs
4 tablespoons butter,
  melted
1 teaspoon cinnamon

Preheat oven to 375°. Mix together and press into bottom of 10-inch springform pan.

Filling:
4 eggs
1 cup sugar
3 (8 oz.) packages cream
  cheese, softened
½ teaspoon almond
  extract
1 teaspoon vanilla extract

Cream eggs and sugar. Gradually add cream cheese. Mixture will be lumpy. Add extracts and mix; pour into pan. Bake 35-40 minutes. Texture is firm except for center. Remove and cool 10 minutes.

Topping:
2 tablespoons sugar
1 teaspoon vanilla extract
½ teaspoon almond
  extract
2 cups sour cream

Increase oven temperature to 400°. Combine ingredients. Pour onto cake; bake 5 minutes. Cool and refrigerate. Flavor is best when made a day ahead.

Raspberry Sauce:
2 (10 oz.) packages
  frozen raspberries
¼ cup orange juice
  concentrate
1 tablespoon cornstarch

Combine ingredients. Cook until thick. Refrigerate. To serve, pour over cake.
        Mrs. Barton Darrow (Ann)

STRAWBERRY PARTY VACHERIN
Serves 8-10

6 egg whites
½ teaspoon cream of
  tartar
1½ cups sugar
¾ cups chopped pecans
2 cups fresh strawberries,
  thinly sliced
2 tablespoons orange
  flavored liqueur
2 cups whipping cream
¼ cup powdered sugar
4 strawberries

Preheat oven to 275°. In large bowl, beat egg whites with cream of tartar until foamy. Gradually add sugar; beat until meringue is stiff and glossy. Fold in nuts. Shape meringue into 4 circles, 7 inches each, on well greased and floured baking sheets. Bake meringues 1 hour 45 minutes. Turn off oven; let meringues cool with oven door closed. Marinate berries 30 minutes in liqueur. Drain well. Whip cream with powdered sugar until stiff. Reserving most attractive layer for top, layer 1 meringue, ⅓ of cream, and ½ of berries; repeat. Top with third meringue. Frost sides with remaining cream. Crumble fourth meringue; press gently into frosted sides. Freeze until firm. Remove from freezer 30 minutes prior to serving. Garnish with whole berries. Easiest to cut with an electric knife.

Mrs. J. W. Capps (Nance)

DACQUOISE AU CHOCOLAT
Serves 10

Meringue:
6 egg whites
⅔ cup sugar
1 cup chopped pecans

Preheat oven to 300°. Grease and flour non-stick baking sheets and outline 3 non-overlapping 9-inch circles, using a cake pan as a guide. Whip egg whites to a froth, gradually beating in sugar. When stiff fold in nuts. Spread meringue mixture evenly over circles; bake 45-55 minutes or until lightly toasted. The meringues must be loosened from the pans before they cool. If centers of layers are not crisp when cool return to oven a few minutes.

Chocolate Butter Cream:
6 egg whites
1¾ cups sugar
2 cups unsalted butter,
  room temperature
3 ounces semi-sweet
  chocolate
Chocolate (garnish)

Place egg whites in top of double boiler and beat until frothy. Put over slightly simmering water and gradually beat in sugar. Increase heat and continue beating until thickened. Mixture should be warm to the touch and sugar completely dissolved. Remove from heat; set in a pan of cold water. Beat until mixture is room temperature. Gradually add butter, beating constantly. Melt chocolate and cool slightly. Blend into butter cream.

To assemble, select the nicest meringue for top layer. Spread each layer with butter cream, stacking one on top of the other. Spread a layer of butter cream on top of dacquoise. Garnish with finely chopped chocolate or chocolate curls.

BOCCONE DOLCE   Serves 8

4 egg whites
⅛ teaspoon salt
¼ teaspoon cream of
tartar
1 cup sugar

Preheat oven to 250⁰. Combine egg whites, salt, and cream of tartar. Beat egg whites until stiff, gradually adding sugar. Cut 3 circular pieces of parchment paper, 8-9 inches in diameter. Smooth meringue on circles and bake 50 minutes until golden. Cool; remove paper while warm. Store in moisture proof container.

Topping:
10 ounces semi-sweet
chocolate
¼ cup hot water
2 cups whipping cream
⅓ cup sugar
1½ pints strawberries,
sliced and drained

Melt chocolate in water. Cool slightly. Whip cream, gradually adding sugar. Layer chocolate mixture, cream, and strawberries over meringues; repeat. Prepare no more than 2 hours before serving. Refrigerate until ready to serve. Slice in wedges to serve.

Mrs. G. Myrph Foote, Jr. (Sila)

Do not make on a humid day.

CANDY BAR COOKIES

Yields 4 dozen

An old bake-off winner

Dough:
¾ cup butter
¾ cup powdered sugar
2 tablespoons whipping cream
1 teaspoon vanilla extract
¼ teaspoon salt
2 cups flour

Preheat oven to 325⁰. Cream butter and sugar. Add cream, vanilla, and salt. Blend in flour. Roll out dough and cut 1 x 1½-inch rectangles. Place on baking sheet. Bake 12-16 minutes.

Caramel Filling:
½ pound vanilla caramels
¼ cup whipping cream
4 tablespoons butter
1 cup powdered sugar
1 cup chopped pecans

In double boiler stir caramels and cream until melted. Remove from heat; add butter, sugar, and pecans.

Chocolate Icing:
1 (6 oz.) package chocolate chips
⅓ cup whipping cream
2 tablespoons butter
1 teaspoon vanilla extract
½ cup powdered sugar

Combine chocolate and cream, melting over low heat. Remove from heat; add butter, vanilla, and sugar. Top baked cookies with caramel filling, chocolate icing and a nut.

Pecan halves

CINNAMON COOKIES

Yields 5-6 dozen

1½ teaspoons cinnamon
Salt
1 teaspoon vanilla extract
6 egg whites, stiffly
  beaten
1 pound powdered sugar
1 pound pecans, chopped

Preheat oven to 325⁰. Sprinkle cinnamon, salt, and vanilla over stiffly beaten egg whites and fold in. Add sugar gradually, folding continuously. Fold in nuts. Line cookie sheets with wax paper; grease and flour paper. Drop batter by teaspoon on paper. Bake 20-25 minutes. Remove carefully while cookies are hot or they will stick to the paper.

DREAM BARS

Yields 3 dozen

Tiny pecan pie squares

1 cup flour
½ cup packed brown
  sugar
½ cup butter, melted

Preheat oven to 375⁰. Combine ingredients. Spread in 5 x 7-inch ovenproof dish. Bake 10 minutes.

Topping:
2 eggs, beaten
1 cup packed brown
  sugar
1 teaspoon vanilla extract
1 cup chopped pecans
2 tablespoons flour
½ teaspoon salt

Combine ingredients; mix well. Spread topping on baked mixture. Reduce heat to 350⁰; bake 20 minutes. Cool. Cut into 1-inch squares.

Mrs. James P. Neill (Geraldine)

ALMOND TOFFEE

Yields 2 dozen

½ cup sliced almonds
1 cup butter
1 cup packed brown
  sugar
½ cup semi-sweet
  chocolate chips
½ cup sliced almonds

Sprinkle almonds in 9 x 13-inch buttered dish. In saucepan combine butter and brown sugar; cook over medium heat, stirring constantly. When mixture reaches 285° on candy thermometer, quickly pour oven almonds. Cool slightly; sprinkle chocolate chips on top. After chocolate chips soften, spread with knife to make even layer; top with almonds. After candy has cooled completely, break into bite-sized pieces and store in airtight container.

Ms. Sheryn R. Jones

MOCHA TRUFFLES

Yields 36

1 (12 oz.) package semi-
  sweet chocolate chips
4 egg yolks
1½ cups powdered sugar
1 cup butter
2 teaspoons instant coffee
  granules
4 tablespoons brandy
2 teaspoons vanilla
  extract
1 cup finely chopped
  pecans

Melt chocolate in double boiler. Beat egg yolks and gradually add powdered sugar. Beat in butter. Dissolve coffee in brandy; add vanilla; combine with egg and butter mixture. Add chocolate; chill several hours. Shape into small balls and roll in nuts. Keep refrigerated until serving.

APRICOT CRESCENTS

Yields 2 dozen

Pastry:
½ cup cottage cheese, drained
½ cup butter
1 cup flour

Preheat oven to 375°. Beat cottage cheese until smooth. Combine with butter and flour to form soft dough. Shape into 1-inch balls. Refrigerate overnight.

Filling:
1 (8 oz.) package dried apricots
1 cup sugar

Place apricots in saucepan with water to cover; cook until tender. Drain; purée, and add sugar. Cool.

Topping:
2 egg whites, beaten until frothy
1 cup finely chopped pecans
1 cup sugar

Roll pastry balls ⅛-inch thick on floured surface. Refrigerate dough you are not working with. Put 1 tablespoon filling in middle of pastry; seal to form a crescent. Combine pecans and sugar. Dip balls into egg whites, then pecan and sugar mixture. Bake on greased baking sheets 12 minutes or until lightly browned.

"A city without a symphony is just a town. It needs the symphony to complete the metropolitan picture no less than it requires a good public school system, a resident university, a medical center, a public library, a seasonal fair..."

John Rosenfield, 1945
Arts Editor
Dallas Morning News

FINGERSKLATSCHEN

Yields 3 dozen

⅔ cup butter
½ cup sugar
2 egg yolks
½ teaspoon almond
    extract
1¾ cups flour
½ teaspoon salt
Red jam or jelly
Powdered sugar

Preheat oven to 325⁰. Cream butter and sugar. Add eggs and almond extract, beating until light. Sift dry ingredients and add to egg mixture. Shape dough in 1-inch balls. Place on baking sheet and press a hole in the center of each. Bake 25 minutes. Cool and fill centers with jam. Sprinkle with powdered sugar.

MACAROON SANDWICHES

Yields 2 dozen

1 pound almond paste
2 cups sugar
4 egg whites

Preheat oven to 325⁰. Line 2-3 baking sheets with unbuttered parchment paper. Mash almond paste; knead in sugar; blend in 3 egg whites plus enough of the remaining egg white to make a soft dough. Drop dough by the teaspoon 2 inches apart. Bake until golden, approximately 25 minutes. Cool on rack. Dampen back of parchment paper to remove cookies. Sandwich with Ganache and set aside to dry.

Ganache:
5 ounces semi-sweet
    chocolate, chopped
2 tablespoons unsalted
    butter, melted
½ cup whipping cream
4 teaspoons crème de
    cacao

Yields 1 cup
Combine chocolate, butter, and cream, mixing until thick and smooth. Remove from heat and add crème de cacao. Chill and stir.

Mrs. Jack Urish (Dee)

SUPER JAM SANDWICHES   Yields 16

2 cups flour
½ cup powdered sugar
¼ teaspoon baking soda
4 tablespoons butter
1 egg yolk
1 teaspoon vanilla extract
Grated rind of 1 lemon
1 egg, beaten
⅓ cup finely chopped
  pecans
¼ cup sugar
¼ cup thick jam

Preheat oven to 350°. Sift together dry ingredients; cut in butter. Beat egg yolk, vanilla, and lemon rind; combine with flour mixture; blend well. Roll dough to thickness of ¼-inch; cut out sixteen 3-inch cookies. Cut ½-inch holes in center of 8 cookies. Place on baking sheet. Paint with beaten egg. Combine nuts and ¼ cup sugar; sprinkle "doughnut" circles only with sugar and nuts. Bake 15-20 minutes or until lightly browned and firm. Sandwich with jam.

Double or triple this recipe so you'll have plenty.

MELTING MOMENTS   Yields 30
Truly melts in your mouth

1 cup butter
⅓ cup powdered sugar
1¼ cups flour
½ cup cornstarch
¼ teaspoon almond
  extract
¼ teaspoon orange
  extract

Glaze:
1 cup powdered sugar,
  sifted
1 tablespoon butter,
  melted
1 tablespoon fresh lemon
  juice
1 tablespoon fresh orange
  juice

Preheat oven to 350°. Cream butter and sugar. Sift in flour and cornstarch; mix. Add extracts, blending thoroughly. Push through cookie press on greased baking sheet. Dough may be chilled, rolled into small balls, and flattened with fingers on baking sheet. Bake 8-10 minutes but do not brown. Glaze while warm.

Mrs. W. Bruce Moore (Susan)

182

ALMOND COOKIES

Yields 48, 2-inch cookies

¾ cup butter, room
  temperature
1 egg
¾ cup sugar
¾ teaspoon almond
  extract
1½ cups self-rising flour
Slivered almonds
  (garnish)
1 egg, beaten

Preheat oven to 350⁰. Combine butter, egg, sugar, and almond extract; mix until well blended. Add flour blending until smooth. Divide dough in half and place on a lightly floured surface. Roll with hands into 2 long cylinders approximately 1¼ inches in diameter. Slice each roll into 24 pieces. Place on baking sheet; top with almonds and brush with egg. Bake 12-14 minutes.

**Mrs. Robert T. Gunby, Jr.
(Elizabeth)**

STAINED GLASS FRUIT FLAN

Serves 10

Pastry base:
6 tablespoons butter
3 tablespoons sugar
5 tablespoons almond
  paste
¾ teaspoon grated lemon
  peel
2 egg whites
1 cup + 2 tablespoons
  flour

Grease and flour a 12-inch flan pan. Cream butter, sugar, almond paste, and lemon peel. Beat in egg whites, then flour. Put into pan; refrigerate 1 hour. Bake at 300⁰ for 50 minutes or until lightly browned. Cool briefly; turn out of pan to finish cooling.

Pastry cream:
1½ cups milk
1 teaspoon vanilla extract
½ cup sugar
¼ cup flour
3-4 eggs, beaten

3 cups soft fruit (berries,
  grapes, bananas,
  melon)
¾ cup apricot jam or
  currant jelly

Scald milk; add vanilla. In top of double boiler over hot water blend sugar, flour, and eggs. Gradually add milk to creamed mixture, stirring until blended. Cook, stirring constantly until it reaches the boiling point. Remove from heat and continue to stir to prevent crusting; cool. Fill pastry with pastry cream and top with fruit of your choice. Brush with warm sieved apricot jam or currant jelly.

CHEDDAR CRUNCH APPLE PIE

Serves 6-8

Filling:
4 cups peeled and sliced
tart apples
1 teaspoon flour
1½ cups sugar
½ teaspoon cinnamon
1 tablespoon butter,
melted

Preheat oven to 375°. Combine all
ingredients and place in prepared crust.

Topping:
½ cup butter
½ cup sugar
1 cup flour
¼ cup grated Cheddar
cheese
½ teaspoon cinnamon

9-inch pie shell, unbaked

Cream butter and sugar. Add flour,
cheese, and cinnamon to mixture.
Sprinkle over pie. Bake 30 minutes.

Mrs. Marjorie B. Waters

*Add ½ cup Cheddar cheese to pastry
dough before rolling out.*

FRENCH APPLE TART

Serves 8

Simply wonderful

Pastry for 10-inch pie
1½ pounds MacIntosh or
Delicious apples,
peeled, cored, and
quartered
2 tablespoons butter
¼ cup sugar
1½ tablespoons powdered
sugar

Preheat oven to 375°. Prepare pastry
dough and chill thoroughly. Roll out
pastry; line 10-inch tart pan. Cut apple
quarters into thin slices. Arrange them
in circular pattern in pan. Dot with
butter and sprinkle with sugar. Bake 50
minutes. After removing tart from pan,
sift with powdered sugar. Serve hot or
cold.

Sprinkle with cinnamon sugar.

ROYAL CHESS PIE
Serves 8

3 eggs
1 cup sugar
1 teaspoon vanilla extract
½ cup butter, melted
⅓ cup buttermilk
1½ cups coconut
1 tablespoon flour
9-inch pie shell, unbaked

Preheat oven to 350°. Blend eggs, sugar, vanilla, butter, buttermilk, coconut, and flour. Pour into pie shell and bake 1 hour.

Topping:
1½ cups whipping cream
⅓ cup sugar
1½ teaspoons vanilla extract
¾ cup sour cream

Beat whipping cream with sugar and vanilla; fold in sour cream. Spread topping on pie.

CHOCOLATE NUT ANGEL PIE
Serves 8

½ cup sugar
¼ teaspoon cream of tartar
2 egg whites, stiffly beaten
1 cup chopped walnuts
1 cup chocolate chips
3 tablespoons hot water
1 teaspoon vanilla extract
1 cup whipping cream, whipped
1 cup chopped pecans
½ cup whipping cream, whipped (garnish)

Preheat oven to 275°. Gradually add sugar and cream of tartar to egg whites. Beat until glossy; fold in nuts. Spoon into buttered 9-inch pie plate. Bake 1 hour. Melt chocolate in saucepan; beat in water. Remove from heat and add vanilla. Cool to room temperature. Fold cream into chocolate mixture; add nuts. Pour into shell; refrigerate several hours or overnight. Garnish with whip cream rosettes.

Mrs. M. Joe Angle (Judy)

FRESH PEACH COBBLER   Serves 6-8

**Pastry for a double crust
  pie
Butter, melted
6 large fresh peaches,
  peeled and sliced
1 cup sugar
1 tablespoon lemon juice
½ teaspoon cinnamon
¼ teaspoon nutmeg
2 tablespoons butter**

Preheat oven to 350°. Roll out pastry
on a floured board. Line ovenproof dish
with dough and brush with melted
butter. Bake 20 minutes. Remove from
oven; fill with mixture of peaches,
sugar, lemon juice, cinnamon, and
nutmeg; criss-cross top with strips of
dough. Sprinkle with cinnamon, dot
with butter. Return to oven and bake
50 minutes. At serving time top each
serving with Maple Cream Sauce.

**Maple Cream Sauce:
1½ cups whipping cream
5 tablespoons maple
  syrup
3 tablespoons light corn
  syrup**

Combine ingredients and bring to a boil
over moderate heat. Cook and stir until
cream is golden and volume is reduced
by half. Serve warm.

Mrs. George M. Pavey, Jr. (Sarah)

PECAN PIE   Serves 6-8

**¾ cup sugar
¾ cup light corn syrup
3 eggs, lightly beaten
4 tablespoons butter,
  melted
1 teaspoon vanilla extract
1½ cups pecan halves
9-inch pie shell, unbaked**

Preheat oven to 375°. Cream sugar and
syrup; add eggs, butter, and vanilla.
Mix well. Stir in pecans. Pour into pie
shell. Bake 15 minutes; reduce heat to
350° and bake 20-25 minutes.

PUMPKIN AIRY PIE

Crust:
1⅓ cups quick or old
   fashioned oats,
   uncooked
⅓ cup packed brown
   sugar
¾ teaspoon cinnamon
⅓ cup butter

Preheat oven to 350°. Combine all ingredients; press into 9-inch pie plate. Place 8-inch pie plate on top and bake 8 minutes. Remove top plate and cool.

Filling:
1 envelope unflavored
   gelatin
⅔ cup packed brown
   sugar
½ teaspoon salt
½ teaspoon cinnamon
½ teaspoon ginger
¼ teaspoon mace
5 egg yolks, lightly
   beaten
¾ cup milk
1 cup cooked pumpkin
3 egg whites
¼ teaspoon cream of
   tartar
⅓ cup sugar
Whipping cream,
   whipped and sweetened

Combine gelatin, brown sugar, salt, cinnamon, ginger, and mace in saucepan. Combine egg yolks and milk; add to dry mixture. Boil 1 minute. Remove from heat and stir in pumpkin; chill. Beat egg whites until foamy; add cream of tartar; gradually add sugar. Continue beating until sugar is dissolved and meringue is glossy. Fold pumpkin mixture into meringue. Pour into cooked crust. Garnish with sweetened whipped cream.

Caroline Schoellkopf
The Compleat Pumpkin Eater

ORANGES ORIENTALE   Serves 8-10
Lightest of all possible desserts

8 large oranges
1 lemon
⅔ cup water
⅔ cup Grand Marnier
1 cup sugar
¼ teaspoon cream of
  tartar

Remove zest from 2 oranges and half of the lemon. Cut into extremely small, narrow strips. Combine all other ingredients in saucepan and bring slowly to a boil, stirring occasionally. Add strips of peel; simmer until volume of syrup is reduced by ⅓. Peel remaining oranges and cut each into 4-5 thin slices. Add juice of lemon to syrup; pour over orange slices. Chill several hours.

STRAWBERRIES
WITH SHERRY CREAM   Serves 8
Calls for crystal

5 egg yolks, beaten
1 cup sugar
1 cup sherry
1 cup whipping cream,
  whipped
3 pints strawberries,
  washed and hulled

Combine eggs, sugar, and sherry in double boiler over hot water; cook until thickened, about 20 minutes. Cool mixture. Shortly before serving fold in whipped cream and ladle over strawberries.

Mrs. Kipp Murray (Gwen)

POACHED PEARS IN WHITE WINE   Serves 4

Syrup:
1½ cups sugar
1½ cups dry white wine
Peel of 1 lemon, cut in
  long strips
2 cinnamon sticks

4 pears, peeled, cored,
  stem intact
Sour cream

Combine syrup ingredients and boil 5 minutes. Place pears upright in deep saucepan; cover and simmer in syrup liquid 30 minutes. Refrigerate pears in syrup. Serve with 2-3 tablespoons syrup and a dollop of sour cream.

ORANGE CREAM IN ORANGE CUPS   Serves 8

8 large naval oranges
   with slice cut off naval
   end
3 cups freshly squeezed
   orange juice
1⅓ cups sugar
2 envelopes unflavored
   gelatin
½ cup cold water
1½ cups whipping cream
½ cup whipping cream,
   whipped
Semi-sweet chocolate,
   grated

Scoop pulp out of oranges. Squeeze pulp to make juice; if necessary, add prepared juice. Flute shells with knife. Stir sugar into juice. Melt gelatin in cold water and simmer in double boiler over hot water until clear. Add gelatin and cream to juice mixture. Spoon into fluted cups. Chill. When ready to serve, top with cream and chocolate. This should be prepared at least 8 hours in advance.

BANANAS CARAMEL   Serves 8-10

1 cup packed brown
   sugar
¼ cup half and half
4 tablespoons butter
1½ teaspoons vanilla
   extract
6 bananas, sliced

Mix brown sugar, half and half, and butter. Cook over low heat, stirring constantly until smooth. Remove from heat; add vanilla. Arrange sliced bananas in dish.

1 cup sour cream
¼ cup powdered sugar

Mix cream and sugar well. Spoon topping over banana mixture and chill before serving. Should be served the same day it is prepared.

Mrs. James C. Hill (Sandy)

COGNAC CHOCOLATE MOUSSE
WITH RASPBERRY SAUCE Serves 8
Dark and delicious

3 ounces semi-sweet
  chocolate
1 ounce unsweetened
  chocolate
¼ cup honey
1½ teaspoons instant
  coffee
1½ tablespoons cognac
1 cup whipping cream,
  whipped
1 (10 oz.) package frozen
  raspberries, puréed and
  strained
½ cup whipping cream,
  whipped
Semi-sweet chocolate

Melt chocolates in double boiler; add honey, coffee, and cognac. Let cool slightly; fold in cream. Pour into 8 individual molds or a 1-quart mold; chill or freeze. For topping, swirl raspberries into whipped cream; sprinkle with chocolate shavings.

Miss Helen Corbitt

MANGO MOUSSE Serves 8
Apricot-colored, tropical fluff

4 ripe mangoes, peeled
  and seeded
⅓ cup fresh lime juice
2 egg whites
Salt
⅓ cup sugar
1 cup whipping cream,
  whipped

Purée mango pulp with lime juice. Beat egg whites and salt; add sugar gradually until stiff meringue forms. Gently fold together mango purée, meringue, and cream. Chill. Make within several hours of serving.

Serve in wine glasses with a lime garnish and rum-soaked pineapple fingers and strawberries on the side.

WHITE MAGIC MOUSSE

Serves 6-8

¼ cup sugar
1 envelope unflavored
   gelatin
1¼ cups milk
4 ounces white chocolate,
   chopped
4 egg yolks, beaten
¼ cup white crème de
   cacao
4 egg whites
2 tablespoons sugar
½ cup whipping cream,
   whipped
White chocolate curls
Fresh strawberries

In saucepan combine ¼ cup sugar and gelatin. Stir in milk; add white chocolate. Cook and stir over low heat until chocolate melts. Gradually stir half of mixture into egg yolks; return to saucepan. Cook and stir 1-2 minutes or until mixture thickens slightly; do not boil. Remove from heat; stir in white crème de cacao. Chill gelatin mixture until partially set, stirring occasionally. Beat egg whites until soft peaks form; gradually add 2 tablespoons sugar, beating until stiff peaks form. Fold into white chocolate along with whipping cream. Attach a buttered foil collar to a buttered and sugared 1-quart soufflé dish. Turn mixture into soufflé dish; chill until firm. To serve, remove collar and garnish with white chocolate curls and strawberries.

PEKING ALMOND CREAM

Serves 6

1 envelope unflavored
   gelatin
¼ cup cold water
¾ cup almond paste
1½ cups milk, scalded in
   double boiler
3 eggs, separated
1 teaspoon vanilla extract
1 cup whipping cream,
   whipped
½ cup sugar
Candied fruit (optional
   garnish)

Soften gelatin in cold water. Add almond paste to milk; stir until blended. Beat egg yolks; add almond milk gradually until mixture is slightly thickened. Add gelatin mixture and vanilla. Chill until partially set. Fold in whipped cream; beat egg whites, adding sugar gradually; fold into almond mixture. Pour into mold or individual glass dishes. Garnish with candied fruit if desired.

At last, a dessert for Chinese meals.

191

COLD APRICOT BAVARIAN
WITH APRICOT SAUCE
Serves 8

2 (17 oz.) cans apricots, drained, seeded, and puréed
4 eggs
3 egg yolks
⅛ teaspoon salt
½ cup sugar
¼ cup cold water
¼ cup lemon juice
2 envelopes unflavored gelatin
½ teaspoon vanilla extract
¼ teaspoon almond extract
2 tablespoons cognac
1 cup whipping cream, lightly whipped

Combine eggs, yolks, salt, and sugar; beat on high speed 15 minutes or until thickened. Add extracts and cognac. Set aside. Mix water, lemon juice, and gelatin; let stand a few minutes to soften. Place in double boiler; cook over low heat, stirring constantly until gelatin is dissolved. Remove from heat. Beat into egg mixture; gently fold in puréed apricots and whipped cream. Turn into buttered 2½-quart soufflé dish. Refrigerate until firm. Unmold on tray of glazed apricots and serve with apricot sauce and chocolate shavings.

Glazed Apricots:
½ cup apricot jam
2 tablespoons water
1 (17 oz.) can apricots, drained, halved, and seeded

Mix apricot jam and water in a saucepan. Cook over low heat; stir over low heat until well blended. On serving tray, arrange apricot halves close together with the open half up. Spread warm sauce over each half with pastry brush.

Apricot Sauce:
1½ cups apricot jam
½ cup water
2 tablespoons sugar
1-2 tablespoons kirsch or other liqueur
Chocolate shavings

Mix jam, water and sugar in saucepan and bring to a boil, stirring constantly. Cook 6-7 minutes; remove from heat. Let cool slightly; press through sieve. Add kirsch to sauce; mix well.

Miss Helen Corbitt

KENTUCKY EGGNOG CHARLOTTE   Serves 10
A Southern comfort!

1 cup butter
2 cups powdered sugar
6 tablespoons whiskey
5 egg yolks, well beaten
5 egg whites, stiffly
   beaten
1 cup chopped pecans
2-3 dozen ladyfingers
2 cups whipping cream,
   whipped

Cream butter and sugar. Combine whiskey and egg yolks; mix well. Add to creamed mixture. Stir in egg whites and nuts. Line 8-inch springform pan with wax paper on sides and bottom. Cover with layer of ladyfingers. Layer ladyfingers and cake mixture; repeat. End with ladyfingers top sides up. Refrigerate 12 hours; frost with whipping cream flavored as desired.

Mrs. John J. DeShazo (Bonner)

COLD LIME SOUFFLÉ MAURICE   Serves 6

1 envelope unflavored
   gelatin
¼ cup water
¾ cup milk
4 egg yolks
½ cup sugar
Juice of 5 limes
1 cup whipping cream,
   whipped
4 drops green food
   coloring
7 egg whites, stiffly
   beaten

Sprinkle gelatin over water to soften. Heat milk in double boiler. Beat egg yolks with sugar until light. Slowly drizzle hot milk over egg yolks, beating constantly to prevent curdling. Return mixture to double boiler; add gelatin. Cook over hot water 10 minutes or until thickened; do not boil. Remove from heat; cool slightly; stir in lime juice. Refrigerate mixture 20 minutes. Combine cream and food coloring; fold into lime mixture; refrigerate until it begins to set. Fold whites gently into lime mixture. Spoon into 1½-quart soufflé dish with wax paper collar; chill at least 3 hours.

193

BLUEBERRY SOUFFLÉ
Serves 6

2 cups blueberries
1 teaspoon lemon juice
1 cup sugar
3 tablespoons water
7 egg whites
½ teaspoon grated lemon
  peel

Preheat oven to 400°. Press 2 cups blueberries through fine strainer, discarding pulp. Sprinkle berry juice with lemon; set aside. Boil sugar with water until syrup spins a thread; soft boil 238°. Stir in blueberry mixture and blend well; cool. Beat egg whites until stiff and add lemon peel. Fold egg whites into blueberry mixture. Turn into buttered and sugared soufflé dish with foil collar; bake 25 minutes. Serve immediately with sauce.

Sauce:
⅓ cup sugar
1½ tablespoons flour
¼ teaspoon salt
1 tablespoon lemon juice
1 cup hot water
1 cup blueberries
2 tablespoons butter

In saucepan combine sugar, flour, and salt. Gradually stir in lemon juice and water. Stir until smooth; cook over medium heat until mixture begins to thicken. Add berries and continue cooking, stirring constantly. Allow to thicken. Remove from heat; beat in butter.

Mrs. W. Bennett Cullum (Betsy)

LEMON SOUFFLÉ
Serves 8

4 eggs, separated
½ cup sugar
**Juice and grated rind of
  1 lemon**
⅛ teaspoon salt
½ cup sugar
Powdered sugar
2 cups sweetened, sliced,
  strawberries

Preheat oven to 325°. Beat yolks until thick; gradually add sugar, lemon juice, and rind. Beat egg whites to a froth; add salt; slowly beat in sugar until meringue stands in stiff peaks. Fold into yolk mixture. Pour into buttered and sugared 1½-quart soufflé dish with foil collar; set in hot water bath. Bake 40 minutes. Dust with powdered sugar and serve immediately with strawberries spooned over top.

CHOCOLATE VELVET
Serves 8

1 envelope unflavored
   gelatin
¼ teaspoon salt
½ cup sugar
½ cup cocoa, sifted
1 cup milk
2 cups whipping cream
½ cup powdered sugar,
   sifted
2 teaspoons vanilla
   extract
¼ teaspoon almond
   extract
Chocolate shavings or
   grated chocolate
1½ cups whipping cream
¼ cup sugar
¼ teaspoon almond
   extract
Candied violets (optional)

In saucepan, combine gelatin, salt, sugar, and cocoa. Add milk; stir 5 minutes over medium heat until gelatin dissolves. Refrigerate 40 minutes. Beat cream, powdered sugar, and extracts until stiff; set aside. Remove cocoa mixture from refrigerator; beat until light and fluffy; fold into cream mixture. Pour into 1-quart soufflé dish with wax paper collar. Refrigerate until firm. At serving time sprinkle with chocolate shavings. Whip cream until stiff, flavoring with sugar and almond extract; dollop around edges of soufflé and crown with candied violets.

SWEET POTATO PUDDING
Serves 12-15

4 large sweet potatoes,
   peeled and finely
   shredded
1 cup buttermilk
2 (13 oz.) cans
   evaporated milk
2 cups sugar
1½ cups butter, melted
1 teaspoon nutmeg
1 teaspoon cinnamon
1 teaspoon baking soda

Preheat oven to 350°. Place sweet potatoes in large, covered ovenproof dish. Pour buttermilk and milk over sweet potatoes immediately after shredding so they will not change color. Stir in sugar, butter, nutmeg, and cinnamon; add baking soda and stir slightly. Bake 1 hour 30 minutes, stirring every 30 minutes. Serve hot.
      Ms. Sheryn R. Jones

For an extra touch, top with whipped cream before serving.

CANTALOUPE ICE
Serves 16-20

4½ cups water
2 cups sugar
3 ripe cantaloupes,
   peeled, seeded, and
   puréed
¾ cup lemon juice
2 egg whites, stiffly
   beaten

Fresh cherries
Brandy

Boil water and sugar 5 minutes; cool. Add cantaloupe, lemon juice, and egg whites. Freeze in 1-gallon ice cream freezer. Marinate cherries in brandy. Place on individual servings.

Mrs. Edward B. Linthicum (Virginia)

SORBET DE CASSIS
Serves 6

9 tablespoons crème de
   cassis
1½ tablespoons lemon
   juice
¼ cup sugar
1 pound fresh or frozen
   blackberries

Blend crème de cassis, lemon juice, and sugar. Add ½ pound blackberries; blend. Add remaining blackberries; pour into shallow dish and freeze. Before serving, pour additional crème de cassis over each portion.

LEMON ICE CREAM
Serves 4-6

2 cups whipping cream
1 cup sugar
1-2 tablespoons grated
   lemon peel
⅓ cup fresh lemon juice

In large bowl, stir together cream and sugar until sugar is thoroughly dissolved. Mix in lemon peel and juice. Pour into sherbet dishes. Freeze several hours until firm.

Mrs. Charles M. Best (Trudy)

FROZEN AVOCADO CREAM   Serves 6

1 large avocado, peeled
and seeded
½ cup orange juice
2 tablespoons lime or
lemon juice
½ cup sugar
1 cup whipping cream
1 cup milk

Purée pulp of avocado and sieve to remove fibers. Combine with remaining ingredients. Freeze in an ice cream freezer or in an ice cube tray in which case mixture must be beaten smooth when partially frozen.

To serve pack avocado cream into orange or lemon shells, refreeze. Present on an ivy-leafed tray with a side order of butter cookies.

FROZEN PUMPKIN BOMBE   Serves 12

2½ cups finely crumbled
ginger snaps
¼ cup sugar
4 tablespoons butter,
melted
1 quart vanilla ice cream,
softened
1 (16 oz.) can pumpkin
1 cup sugar
½ teaspoon salt
1 teaspoon cinnamon
½ teaspoon ginger
¼ teaspoon cloves
1 teaspoon vanilla extract
1 cup whipping cream,
stiffly whipped
Whipping cream,
whipped (optional)
Cherries (optional)

For layer 1, combine crumbs, ¼ cup sugar, and butter; reserve 1 cup crumb mixture. Press remaining crumb mixture evenly inside 2½-quart mixing bowl lined with wax paper or foil. Mold into shape by pressing 1½-quart bowl into center. Place crumb-lined bowl in freezer.
For layer 2, pack ice cream inside frozen crumbs, using chilled 1½-quart bowl again as a mold. Freeze until ice cream hardens.
For layer 3, combine pumpkin, 1 cup sugar, salt, and spices; stir in whipping cream and vanilla. Pour mixture into center of ice cream. Top evenly with remaining 1 cup crumbs. Freeze. To serve, unmold and invert on serving platter. Thaw slightly at room temperature. Garnish with cream and cherries. Cut into wedges.

Mrs. Billie Redd

GRAND MARNIER PUFFS

Yields 3 dozen

1 cup water
½ cup butter
¼ teaspoon salt
1 cup flour
4 eggs
Crème patisserie
Powdered sugar

Preheat oven to 425⁰. Combine water, butter, and salt; bring to boil. Remove from heat; add flour all at once, stirring vigorously until mixture leaves sides of pan and forms a ball. If no ball forms, place over low heat and beat briskly a few minutes. Cool 5 minutes. Add eggs, 1 at a time, beating until mixture is smooth and glossy. Drop by teaspoons on greased baking sheet 2 inches apart. Bake 15 minutes. Reduce temperature to 350⁰ and bake 8 minutes. Before serving cut off top and fill with crème patisserie. Replace top and sprinkle with powdered sugar.

Crème Patisserie:
¾ cup sugar
7 egg yolks
⅓ cup flour
⅛ teaspoon salt
2 cups milk, scalded
1½ teaspoons vanilla
  extract
3 orange rinds, grated
1-2 tablespoons Grand
  Marnier

Combine sugar and egg yolks beating until fluffy. Add flour and salt gradually, beating well. Gradually add milk to yolk mixture. Cook over low heat until thickened, stirring constantly. Remove from heat; stir in vanilla, orange rind, and Grand Marnier. Cover with plastic wrap, pressing into surface to prevent crusting. Chill well. Fill as directed.

An elegant ending for a dinner party.

CREAM CHEESE CRÊPES
WITH APRICOT SAUCE
Serves 4

8 crêpes

Filling:
1 (8 oz.) package cream cheese, room temperature
¼ cup butter, room temperature
¼ cup sugar
1½ teaspoons vanilla extract
½ teaspoon almond extract
1 teaspoon grated lemon rind

Preheat oven to 350⁰. Mix all ingredients until light and fluffy. Spread each crêpe almost to the edge with some of the cheese filling. Fold 2 ends of the crêpes and roll. Place crêpes in a buttered oven proof dish and dot with butter. Bake crêpes 10 minutes.

Sauce:
⅔ cup apricot jam
⅓ cup orange juice
2 tablespoons butter
1 tablespoon lemon juice
1½ teaspoons grated orange or lemon rind
1 tablespoon Grand Marnier
6 tablespoons sliced almonds, toasted (garnish)

Combine all ingredients except almonds in a saucepan. Heat sauce slowly, stirring until smooth and slightly thickened. Spoon sauce over crêpes. Sprinkle with almonds.

INDEX

Avocado Asparagus Mold, 57
Chicken Avocado Salad, 63
Cold Carrot Soup with
    Avocado, 40
Frozen Avocado Cream, 197
Avocado and Carrot Salad, 52
Avocado Asparagus Mold, 57

B
Bagels, 151
Baked Chicken Strips, 84
Baked Ham with Cumberland
    Sauce, 105
Banana Punch, 32
Bananas Caramel, 189
Barbeque Shrimp, 81
Basil Dressing, 66
Basil, Fresh
    Baked Chicken Strips, 84
    Basil Dressing, 66
    Basil-Pineapple Jelly, 158
    Greek Salad, 51
    Herb Butters, 158
    Herb Rice, 134
    Herb Vinegar, 69
    Herbed Lamb Chops, 111
    Herbloody Merrie, 34
    Linguine with Zucchini and
        Pesto Sauce, 116
    Opal Basil Marinated
        Mushrooms, 23
Basil-Pineapple Jelly, 158
Bay, Fresh
    Herb Rice, 134
Beans
    Cuban Black Bean Soup, 41
    Great Green Beans, 123
    Seven Bean Soup, 45
    Tangy Green Beans, 124
Beef
    Beef Madeira, 94
    Beef Tenderloin Stuffed with
        Mushrooms, 95
    Beef with Mustard Sauce, 95
    Bleu Cheese Flank Steak, 94

Burgundy Beef Brochette, 97
    Green Chili Flank Steak, 98
    Shanghai Skewered Steak, 100
    South Sea Beef, 101
    Southwestern Chalupas, 99
    Steak Au Poirre, 98
    Steak Diane, 97
    Swedish Pot Roast, 100
    Wine-Sauced Beef Tenderloin,
        96
Beef Madeira, 94
Beef Tenderloin Stuffed with
    Mushrooms, 95
Beef with Mustard Sauce, 95
Beverages
    Almond Tea, 31
    Amaretto Eggnog, 31
    Banana Punch, 32
    Christmas Buttered Rum, 32
    Citrus Slush, 31
    Coffee Cream Punch, 32
    Herbloody Merrie, 34
    Hilltop's Herbal Wine Punch,
        34
    Holiday Punch, 33
    Italian Wine Pitcher, 33
    Mint Punch, 33
Biscuits
    Cheese Biscuits, 17
    Grandma's Biscuits, 150
Black Forest Cake, 162
Blackberry
    Sorbet De Cassis, 196
Bleu Cheese Flank Steak, 94
Bleu Cheese with Chives
    Dressing, 66
Bleu Crab Fondue, 17
Blueberry Soufflé, 194
Boccone Dolce, 176
Borage Flowers, Fresh
    Frankfurt's Green Sauce, 67
    Herb Butters, 158
    Hilltop's Herbal Wine Punch,
        34
Braised Leeks and Cream, 129
Breads
    Bagels, 151

203

214

Wheat, Cracked Carrot Bread, 154
White Magic Mousse, 191

Wine
    Hilltop's Herbal Wine Punch, 34
    Italian Wine Pitcher, 33
Wine-Sauced Beef Tenderloin, 96

Y
Yogurt
    Greek Chicken With Yogurt, 86
    Spinach-Yogurt Dip, 21

Z
Zucchini
    Creamy Zucchini Soup, 47
    Linguine with Zucchini and Pesto Sauce, 116
    Sesame Zucchini, 140
    Zucchini and Mushroom Fettucine, 17
    Zucchini Provençal, 141
    Zucchini with Parmesan, 141
Zucchini and Mushroom Fettuccine, 17
Zucchini Provençal, 141
Zucchini with Parmesan, 141

PRESENTING A TASTY COMPOSITION
DALLAS SYMPHONY SWEETS

Each magnificent bonbon is composed of a
soft coffee center, hand dipped in the
finest dark chocolate, made with the
purest all natural ingredients,
without preservatives. Also
available in milk chocolate.

And introducing a fine assortment of chocolates packaged especially
for the new season!

TO ORDER:

Contact Dallas Symphony Sweets
P.O. Box 795332
Dallas, Texas 75379-5332

(214) 630-2651

DSOL-Junior Group Publications
P.O. Box 8472
Dallas, Texas 75205

Please send _____ copies of **THE DALLAS SYMPHONY COOKBOOK.**

Price $12.95
Postage and handling 2.00
(Texas residents add tax) 65

Total per book $_____ Total enclosed $_____

Please send _____ copies of **NOTED COOKERY** @ $12.95, plus $2.00 for postage and handling. (Texas residents add $.65 per book for state tax.)

Make checks payable to **THE DALLAS SYMPHONY COOKBOOK.**

Name _____

Address _____

City, State, Zip _____

DSOL-Junior Group Publications
P.O. Box 8472
Dallas, Texas 75205

Please send _____ copies of **THE DALLAS SYMPHONY COOKBOOK.**

Price $12.95
Postage and handling 2.00
(Texas residents add tax) 65

Total per book $_____ Total enclosed $_____

Please send _____ copies of **NOTED COOKERY** @ $12.95, plus $2.00 for postage and handling. (Texas residents add $.65 per book for state tax.)

Make checks payable to **THE DALLAS SYMPHONY COOKBOOK.**

Name _____

Address _____

City, State, Zip _____

ORDER BOOKS HERE

DSOL-Junior Group Publications
P.O. Box 8472
Dallas, Texas 75205

ease send _____ copies of **THE DALLAS SYMPHONY COOKBOOK.**

Price $12.95
Postage and handling 2.00
(Texas residents add tax) 65

`otal per book $_____ Total enclosed $_____

lease send _____ copies of **NOTED COOKERY** @ $12.95,
us $2.00 for postage and handling. (Texas residents add $.65 per book
r state tax.)

1ake checks payable to **THE DALLAS SYMPHONY COOKBOOK.**

`ame _____

ddress _____

ity, State, Zip _____

- -

DSOL-Junior Group Publications
P.O. Box 8472
Dallas, Texas 75205

ease send _____ copies of **THE DALLAS SYMPHONY COOKBOOK.**

Price $12.95
Postage and handling 2.00
(Texas residents add tax) 65

`otal per book $_____ Total enclosed $_____

lease send _____ copies of **NOTED COOKERY** @ $12.95,
lus $2.00 for postage and handling. (Texas residents add $.65 per book
r state tax.)

1ake checks payable to **THE DALLAS SYMPHONY COOKBOOK.**

`ame _____

ddress _____

ity, State, Zip _____

ORDER BOOKS HERE